Sensational Settings

Over 80 Ways to Arrange Your Quilt Blocks

REVISED EDITION

JOAN HANSON

Martingale®
& COMPANY

Sensational Settings: Over 80 Ways to Arrange Your Quilt Blocks, Revised Edition
© 1993, 2004 by Joan Hanson

First Edition 1993
Revised Edition 2004

That Patchwork Place® is an imprint of Martingale & Company®.

Martingale & Company
20205 144th Avenue NE
Woodinville, WA 98072-8478
www.martingale-pub.com

CREDITS

President . . . . Nancy J. Martin
CEO . . . . Daniel J. Martin
Publisher . . . . Jane Hamada
Editorial Director . . . . Mary V. Green
Managing Editor . . . . Tina Cook
Technical Editor . . . . Cyndi Hershey
Copy Editor . . . . Liz McGehee
Design and Production Manager . . . . Stan Green
Illustrator . . . . Laurel Strand
Cover Designer . . . . Regina Girard
Text Designer . . . . Jennifer LaRock Shontz
Photographer . . . . Brent Kane

Printed in China
09 08 07 06 05 04   8 7 6 5 4 3 2 1

MISSION STATEMENT
Dedicated to providing quality products and service to inspire creativity

ACKNOWLEDGMENTS

I would like to thank the following talented and creative quilters who graciously shared their inspiring quilts in this book: Alice Berg, Sandy Bonsib, Elizabeth Hamby Carlson, Mary Covey, Mimi Dietrich, Mary Hickey, Virginia Kennedy, Janet Kime, Robin Korth, Nancy J. Martin, Frieda Martinis, Chris Mewhinney, Deborah J. Moffett-Hall, Cleo Nollette, Jo Parrott, Susan Phillips, Judy Pollard, Sally Schneider, Pat Speth, Robin Strobel, George Taylor, Jane Townswick, Jean Van Bockel, and Mary Ellen Von Holt. A special thank you to Penny McMorris and the Electric Quilt Company for their contribution to the section on designing with quilting software. Creativity and a willingness to share are the things that make quilters such wonderful people and special friends. I am grateful to and humbled by each of you.

Library of Congress Cataloging-in-Publication Data

Hanson, Joan
    Sensational settings : over 80 ways to arrange your quilt blocks / Joan Hanson.—Rev. ed.
        p.   cm.
    ISBN 1-56477-521-6
  1. Patchwork—Patterns. 2. Quilting—Patterns. I. Title.
    TT835.H337 2004
    746.46'041—dc22

                                2003021768

Contents

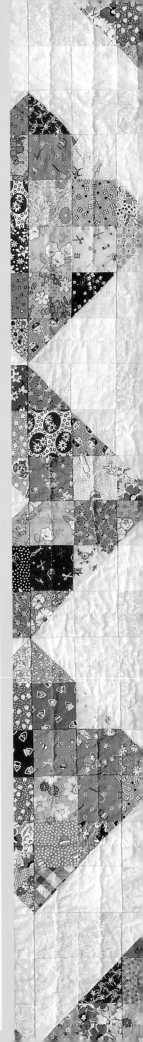

Introduction

WE ALL KNOW ONE WHEN WE SEE ONE, a quilt that reaches out and speaks to us, asking us to linger and enjoy its beauty for just a little longer. In this book, we'll explore ways to set quilt blocks together in a pleasing overall design and so create a stunning quilt that is a joy to behold.

Since I first wrote about the challenges of setting quilt blocks 10 years ago, I have probably made close to 100 quilts. I still enjoy finding the perfect solution to setting a group of quilt blocks together. Each project comes with its own personality and design considerations, and designing a quilt for a set of blocks that shows them off to their best advantage is a truly rewarding experience.

Even though it's been 10 years since the first edition of this book, a few setting dilemmas have stayed the same: a set of blocks isn't always a consistent size; sometimes a large quilt needs to be made out of a small number of blocks; occasionally there are an awkward number of blocks, such as 10, 13, or 22, to use; and sometimes blocks don't have a unifying color theme. The setting solutions that worked several years ago are still just as useful today. As you look at the quilts on the pages of this book, I hope that you will be inspired by the creative efforts of talented quilters who have solved many design challenges, and that you will find the perfect solution for your set of blocks.

For me, designing a setting and choosing fabrics are among the most exciting and important steps in producing a stunning quilt. In this book, quilt settings are divided into categories, with different quilts to illustrate the different options and give you inspiration. You'll notice that each quilt photo contains outlined areas. This is to help you readily identify the areas of the quilt that are being discussed in the text. Since this is a design book and not a pattern book, space doesn't allow instructions for each quilt shown. All the quilts (and the instructions for making them) appear in other Martingale & Company books. Just turn to the resources on page 77 if you'd like to locate the book with instructions for making a particular quilt.

Once you have ideas to work with, it's time to do some designing. If you're the pencil and graph paper type, you'll find a step-by-step plan to get you started. If you're the computer type, there is a section on using quilt-design software. Whichever method you prefer, this book will enable you to start cutting and stitching your way to the quilt of your dreams.

Sometimes, after working your way through the planning stage, you'll decide not to make a particular quilt. Consider the time well spent, as you will have made that decision before investing effort and fabric in a quilt that might have been a disappointment.

When you start a project, you'll probably have one or more "givens" with which to work. Perhaps the finished quilt needs to be a certain size to cover a particular bed or wall space, or you have a given number of blocks and want to include all of them in the quilt. You can plan a quilt setting that will stretch blocks to cover a bigger area or one that will squeeze them into a smaller one.

Many variables come into play when you decide how to set blocks into a quilt. Some blocks must be set horizontally, such as House blocks, while other blocks are designed for a diagonal set, also called "on point." Many Basket blocks are set on point, for example. A variety of blocks, such as Star blocks, can be oriented either horizontally or diagonally, with dramatically different results. As a general rule, remember that horizontal lines are calming and restful, while diagonal lines give movement and add drama to your design.

The choice is yours. Don't hesitate to branch out and set a quilt in a way you haven't tried before. It's easier than you may think! As you look through the settings that follow, consider them a beginning, a starting point for sparking your own ideas. Try combining elements of several settings to come up with your own variations. Remember, there are no hard and fast rules here. Some of the best quilt settings are just waiting to be tried, so don't hesitate to break out and reach for them.

◄ The straight rows of "Spring Flower Garden" are visually soothing, with the gentle curve of the flower tops providing just a little movement.

▶ The diagonal lines in "Garden Path" create a dynamic sense of motion.

Getting Started

MANY MORE ELEMENTS THAN QUILT BLOCKS make up a quilt. Since these elements will be mentioned throughout this book, it's important to be familiar with them. Study the illustration and the definitions that follow. If a quilt element is commonly known by more than one term, alternative names are given in parentheses.

Alternating plain block: A block made out of a single, whole piece of fabric. Alternating plain blocks are placed between stitched blocks. In assembled quilts, they're often embellished with an elaborate quilting pattern.

Alternating design block: A pieced or appliquéd block that is placed between the main stitched blocks. Alternating design blocks usually connect visually with the main blocks to move a design across the quilt.

Appliqué block: A design made up of small (usually curved) pieces that are stitched by hand or machine onto a larger background block.

Appliqué border: A design made up of small (usually curved) pieces that are stitched by hand or machine onto long strips that form the border of the quilt.

Backing (lining): A large piece of fabric that covers the back of a quilt. The backing may need to be seamed together from two or more pieces of fabric to accommodate a large quilt.

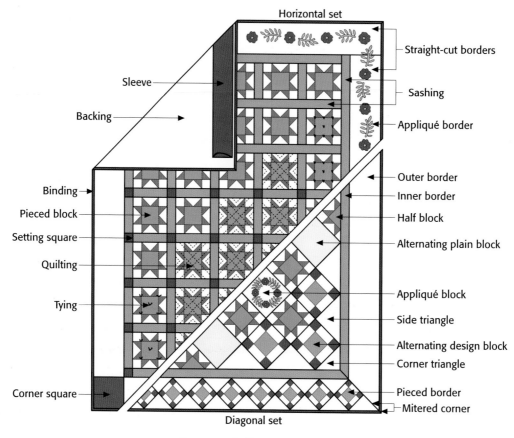

Common Quilt Terms

Batting (not shown in illustration): A layer inside the quilt, sandwiched between the quilt top and the quilt backing. It is usually fluffy cotton, polyester, wool, or silk (or some combination thereof) that adds warmth and, after quilting, texture to the quilt.

Binding: A strip of fabric, cut on either the straight of grain or the bias, that is stitched to the edge of a quilt to cover the raw edges.

Block: Usually a square or rectangular design unit that is pieced or appliquéd. Typically, quilt tops are made by repeating one or more quilt blocks in a pleasing arrangement.

Border: The area surrounding the main body of the quilt top. It acts like a frame on a picture to enhance the design. The border may be a pieced or appliquéd design, or both, or it may be made of one or more strips of unpieced fabric of varying widths.

Corner square: A square of fabric sometimes used to join adjacent border strips.

Corner triangle (corner setting triangle): A triangle used to fill in the four corners of a diagonally set quilt before the borders (if any) are added. Corner triangles should be half-square triangles, which are made by cutting a square in half once diagonally. In half-square triangles, the straight grain of the fabric runs along the short edges and the bias along the long edge. Half-square triangles are used at corners to keep the fabric straight grain at the quilt edges, thereby minimizing stretching and distortion.

Diagonal setting (on-point setting): A design arranged so that the blocks are pieced together in diagonal rows, with side and corner triangles added to complete the rows.

Framed block (not shown in illustration): A block surrounded by a border. Frames can be straight, or tilted with triangles added to each side. Frames are not to be confused with sashing.

Half block: Half of a design unit, used to fill in a diagonally set quilt at the side, top, and/or bottom edges to create a straight edge.

Horizontal setting (straight setting): A design arranged so that the blocks and other components are arranged in straight rows.

Mitered corner: A point where three seams intersect at an angle to form a Y shape.

Pieced block: Small pieces of fabric, of various shapes, stitched together by hand or machine to form a larger design.

Pieced border: A design made up of small shapes stitched together into long strips to form the border of a quilt.

Quilt top: The upper layer of a quilt, usually appliquéd or pieced to form an overall design. The quilt top can be made up of any combination of blocks, sashing strips, setting squares, and borders.

Sashing (lattice): A single strip of fabric, or a pieced strip, sewn between rows of blocks.

Setting square (corner post, set square, sashing square): A square of fabric at the intersection of two sashing pieces. The setting square could be one piece of fabric, or it could be pieced or appliquéd.

Side triangle (edge triangle or side setting triangle): A triangle used to fill in the side, top, or bottom edges of a diagonally set quilt to create a straight edge. Side triangles should be quarter-square triangles, which are made by cutting a square in half twice diagonally. In quarter-square triangles, the straight grain of the fabric runs along the long side of the triangle and the bias along the short edges. Keeping the straight-of-grain at the quilt edges stabilizes the quilt and minimizes stretching along the edges.

Sleeve (rod pocket): A tube of fabric attached to the backing at the upper edge of a quilt so that a hanging rod or dowel can be inserted.

Straight-cut border: A border that is applied to the quilt top in two steps. First, border strips are stitched to two opposite sides (usually the longest sides). Then the remaining borders are stitched to the quilt and to the previously attached borders. The two sets of borders butt against each other rather than meeting at an angle, as in a mitered corner.

Setting Options

LET'S EXPLORE THE ENDLESS CHOICES for setting your blocks together. As you start to think about how to proceed, consider what it is you want to accomplish with the blocks you are working with. Answering some basic questions will narrow your focus on the design possibilities. How will the quilt be used? In other words, does it need to be a certain size? (Do you have just a few blocks that need to become a large quilt?) Does the quilt need to cover a bed or fit a wall space? Is it going to be a baby quilt or given to a young child? (Do you need to make a quick quilt that will stand up to the daily use of a toddler?) Is it a wedding gift that you hope will become a treasured heirloom? (Do you want a quilt that will show off your best work and be admired for years to come?) Are you making an anniversary quilt for a couple in your family that many family members will contribute a block to? Are you making a quilt for a school project that students will be involved in? Is it a friendship quilt, with all the blocks made by different people? Or do you have a set of blocks passed down from a beloved grandmother that you would like to make into a quilt?

Some of the goals you want to accomplish might be: making just a few blocks stretch into a large quilt; unifying differently colored blocks into an overall, pleasing color scheme; setting together an odd number of blocks (such as 13, 17, or 22—numbers that don't fall into the three across and four down or five across and seven down category). And then there's one of my favorite situations, blocks that are not all the same size. Since life is rarely simple and straightforward, you may even have several of the aforementioned design challenges to deal with in one quilt. For me, this is where the real fun of making quilts begins! So let's take a look at some options for arranging quilt blocks. I've divided the alternatives into eight categories, but these are somewhat arbitrary, and many quilt designs combine elements of two or more categories in the same quilt.

Blocks, Blocks, and More Blocks

FIRST, LET'S TAKE A LOOK AT ALL THE setting variations that use only combinations of blocks, without sashing strips, setting squares, or other elements. In addition to setting the same block side by side, you can also alternate pieced blocks with plain squares or with other pieced or appliquéd blocks. Or you might combine two or three different blocks to create endless secondary designs. What fun it is to audition blocks and consider all these possibilities. If you're thinking only about horizontally set blocks, don't forget to consider diagonal arrangements and see how your blocks will look on-point.

Side-by-Side Blocks

THE SIMPLEST WAY OF SETTING BLOCKS together, and the first one that comes to mind, is just lining them up in neat rows and sewing them together. We're used to organizing things this way, as with books on a shelf or cans of soup in a cupboard. There are many instances in which setting blocks side by side will be your best option.

Many blocks that you might want to include in the same quilt can be set side by side, as long as the blocks are fairly consistent in size.

▶ Side-by-side blocks: "Millennium Star" by Robin Korth, 2000, Davenport, Iowa, 72½" x 96½".

Corner Designs

Some blocks have corner elements that create a secondary pattern when the blocks are placed side by side. In the following illustration, the green stars are the secondary pattern. When using corner elements to create a secondary design, try using slightly different shades of the same color in opposite corners so that, when the blocks are sewn together, the pieces will contrast slightly rather than blend together. In the illustration, notice that white background pieces are substituted for green ones at the outer edges, lightening the edges of the pieced interior and keeping the focus on the stars.

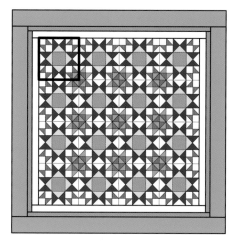

Let's take a look at the same block set diagonally. The straight-set quilt used sixteen blocks. The on-point version shown below uses thirteen blocks along with pieced corner and side setting triangles. Turned on point, this block has a whole new look. Which do you like best?

Scrappy Blocks

Scrappy blocks in which the background fabric changes from block to block work well because the values are the same but the fabrics are different, allowing each block to shine on its own while connecting with its neighbors.

Scrappy blocks set side by side: "Stars and Stripes" by Mary Ellen Von Holt, 2001, Marietta, Georgia, 24½" x 30½".

Value Changes

One way to add visual interest to a side-by-side setting is to change the colors from light in the middle of the quilt to dark at the edges. The blocks at the edges of "White and Blue, Old and New" form a very simple border.

Secondary Patterns

Many blocks gain an unexpected graphic punch when set side by side. A secondary pattern emerges as the boundary of one block blurs with its neighbors, causing a new design to appear. In "Daniel's Boon," careful placement of lights and darks makes the blocks appear to weave together.

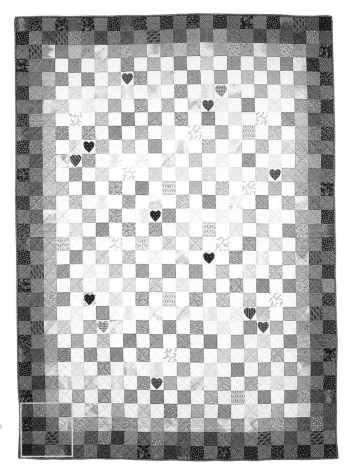

Secondary patterns in blocks set side by side: "Daniel's Boon" by Deborah J. Moffet-Hall, 2000, Hatfield, Pennsylvania, 38½" x 44".

Value changes in blocks set side by side: "White and Blue, Old and New" by Mary Hickey, 1995, Keyport, Washington, 72½" x 96½". Hand quilted by the Amish of Millersburg, Ohio.

Symmetrical and Asymmetrical Blocks

Symmetrical blocks are the same at all four sides. If you divided a symmetrical block into quarters, all four quarters would look the same; they'd just be rotated. Most Star blocks are symmetrical. Asymmetrical blocks form a mirror image when folded in half diagonally—that is, when divided once from corner to corner—so that the two sides are the same. Log Cabin and Jacob's Ladder are asymmetrical blocks.

When looked at individually, asymmetrical blocks don't always seem inspiring, but when they are set side by side, wonderful designs begin to pop out. Try combining asymmetrical blocks and turning them in different directions to create a variety of designs. The old-time favorite settings for Log Cabin blocks—Barn Raising, Light and Dark, Streak of Lightning, Straight Furrows, Sunshine and Shadows, and Pinwheel—are accomplished in this way.

Sawtooth Star

Monkey Wrench or Shoo Fly

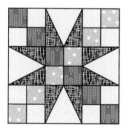

54-40 or Fight

Rambler

Symmetrical Blocks

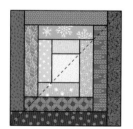

Log Cabin

Buckeye Beauty

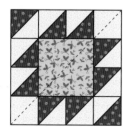

Hovering Hawks

Jacob's Ladder

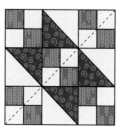

Asymmetrical Blocks

Asymmetrical blocks in a **Light and Dark** setting: "Sunshine and Shadow" by Nancy J. Martin and Cleo Nollette, 2000, Woodinville, Washington, 76½" x 76½". Quilted by Anna Stutzman.

◄ Asymmetrical blocks in a Medallion setting: "Perkiomen Valley in the 1930s" by Susan Phillips, 2000, Fairbanks, Alaska, 70" x 70".

▶ Asymmetrical blocks in a Barn Raising setting: "Winter in the Cabin" by Joan Hanson, 1993, Seattle, Washington, 73" x 94". Quilted by Laura Raber.

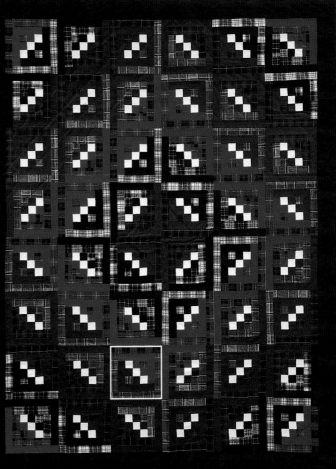

◀ Asymmetrical blocks set side by side: "Cheerful Child" by Mary Hickey, 1993, Seattle, Washington, 87" x 87". Quilted by the Amish.

▶ Asymmetrical blocks in a Straight Furrows setting: "Beach Blues" by Joan Hanson, 2000, Seattle, Washington, 45½" x 57½".

▶ Asymmetrical blocks set side by side: "North Wind" by Mary Hickey, 2000, Seattle, Washington, 70½" x 70½". Hand quilted by Anna Hostetler.

Now try adding some color changes and things really get interesting! Using the same block in two color variations increases your design options. For example, blue strips in some blocks and green strips in others makes Flying Geese blocks in "Flying Geese Fishing Quilt" seem to interweave.

◀ Asymmetrical blocks with color variations: "Flying Geese Fishing Quilt," designed and pieced by Joan Hanson, 63" x 76". Quilted by Dawn Kelly.

Appliqué Blocks

The side-by-side setting is very effective with appliqué blocks that "float" on the background fabric. To produce the floating effect, just use the same background fabric for each block. When the blocks are sewn together, a portion of background fabric will remain between the appliqué designs, floating them against the common background. What a difference the choice of a background fabric makes in the two lovely appliqué quilts shown below and on the next page.

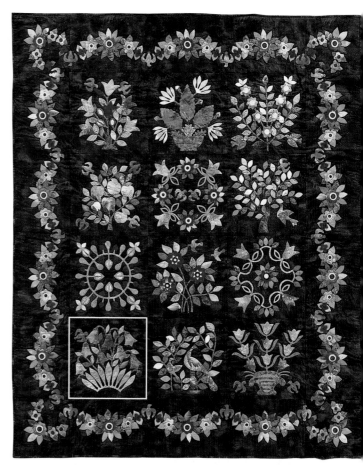

Appliqué blocks set side by side: "Pennsylvania Flower Garden," designed by Jane Townswick, 62" x 76". Machine appliquéd by Gail Kessler, 2000, Oley, Pennsylvania. Machine quilted by Carol Singer.

Appliqué blocks set side by side: "Garden Comfort" by Mimi Dietrich, 2002, Baltimore, Maryland, 78½" x 94½". Machine quilted by Linda Newsom.

Consider side-by-side settings for:

- Asymmetrical blocks, such as Log Cabin, Contrary Wife, and Jacob's Ladder
- Blocks that form a secondary design when placed next to each other
- Appliqué blocks that would float against a common background fabric

Alternating Design Blocks with Plain Blocks

IF YOU HAVE A LIMITED NUMBER of blocks and want to stretch them into a large quilt, alternating your design blocks with plain square blocks might do the trick. Just remember that all those plain blocks will probably require a greater amount of quilting. The time you don't spend piecing additional blocks will be spent quilting later.

To end up with the same block in all four corners of a horizontally set quilt with alternating blocks, you'll need an odd number of blocks in each row and an odd number of rows.

Matching Backgrounds

Many blocks connect visually at the corners, adding diagonal movement to a quilt when alternated with a plain block. One example is a simple Nine Patch block that alternates with a plain block, with both blocks using the same background fabric. When you use the same background fabric for the plain square as for your design blocks, the blocks appear to float on the surface of the quilt.

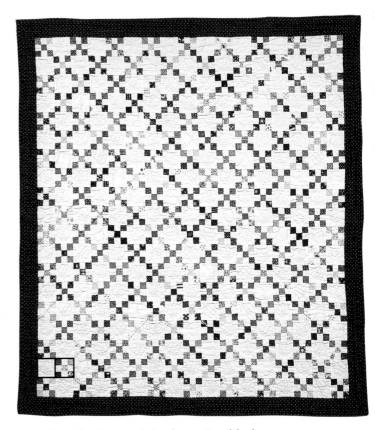

Matching backgrounds in alternating blocks: "Mark's Nine Patch" by the members of Needle and I, 1991, Seattle, Washington, 57" x 63".

Contrasting Backgrounds

Plain blocks cut from a contrasting fabric can also be a good choice when you want to show off design blocks to their best advantage. Using a contrasting fabric for the alternating blocks defines the edges of the blocks and lets each one stand out.

Novelty Prints

Plain blocks are great spots for large-scale patterns, such as florals and novelty prints. A Puss in the Corner block combined with a juvenile print in the alternating block can be a quick project and an adorable baby quilt.

◀ Contrasting backgrounds in alternating blocks: "Maggie's Quilt" by George Taylor, 42" x 56½". Collection of Maggie French; photo by Sharon Risedorph.

▶ Novelty prints as alternate blocks: "Kids in the Corner" by Joan Hanson, 1998, Seattle, Washington, 35½" x 45½". From the collection of Travis Wrigley.

On-Point Setting

Alternating blocks set on-point have a liveliness all their own. Basket blocks, Heart blocks, and many appliqué blocks are oriented on the diagonal and look best set this way. Again, the alternating block can match or contrast with the background of the primary block. Notice, too, that corner and side setting triangles are needed to complete the edges of the rows. See page 74 to read about measuring and cutting side and corner triangles.

In "Wonder Baby," below left, the primary blocks float against a background.

In "Barbie's Baskets," below right, a contrasting fabric in the alternating blocks defines each primary block.

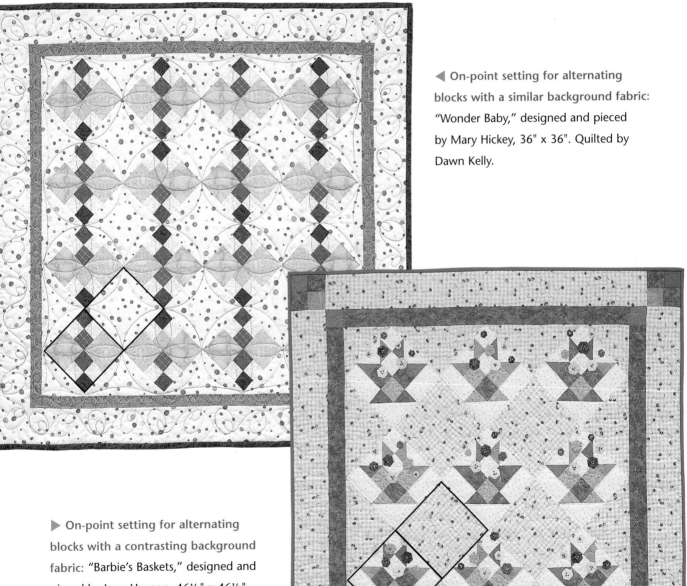

◀ On-point setting for alternating blocks with a similar background fabric: "Wonder Baby," designed and pieced by Mary Hickey, 36" x 36". Quilted by Dawn Kelly.

▶ On-point setting for alternating blocks with a contrasting background fabric: "Barbie's Baskets," designed and pieced by Joan Hanson, 46½" x 46½". Quilted by Dawn Kelly.

Background As Border

Taking this one step further, the center alternating blocks can blend with the main blocks, and the side and corner triangles can change to a contrasting fabric to form an inner border, as in "Red Union Square."

Scrappy Squares

You could also try making all the alternating squares, side triangles, and corner triangles with multiple fabrics for a scrappy look. If you like buying fat quarters and half yards of fabric, this is a good way to use them.

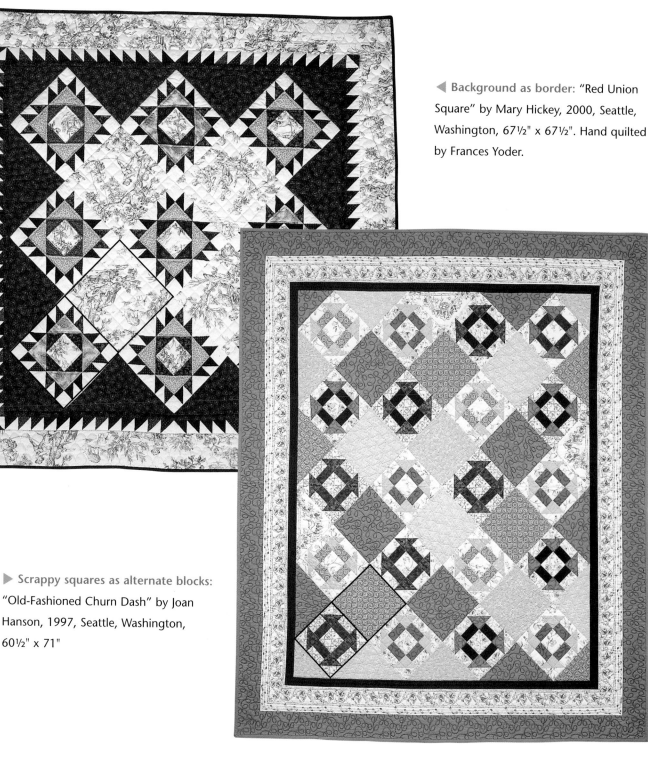

◀ Background as border: "Red Union Square" by Mary Hickey, 2000, Seattle, Washington, 67½" x 67½". Hand quilted by Frances Yoder.

▶ Scrappy squares as alternate blocks: "Old-Fashioned Churn Dash" by Joan Hanson, 1997, Seattle, Washington, 60½" x 71"

Scrappy squares as alternate blocks: "My Heart Belongs to the '30s" by Sandy Bonsib, 1999, Issaquah, Washington, 39½ x 47¾". Quilted by Becky Kraus.

Quilting Options

Some quilters view the alternating plain blocks as blank canvas and like to enhance them with elaborate quilting. In a high-contrast quilt like the one shown below, intricate quilting in the plain blocks can balance the pieced blocks to form a pleasing overall design.

Quilting options for alternating plain blocks: "Winter Lilies" by Jo Parrott, 71" x 71".

Consider alternating plain-block settings for:
- Nine Patch or other designs that connect at the corners to create diagonal movement
- Complex pieced or appliquéd blocks
- A small number of blocks that you'd like to stretch into a relatively big quilt
- Elaborate quilting in combination with pieced blocks

Alternating Design Blocks

INTERESTING DESIGNS OCCUR when two different pieced or appliquéd blocks are used in combination. Usually one of the blocks is more complex than the other and, if pieced, both blocks typically use the same grid divisions so that some of the intersections line up and carry the eye across the design.

Simple Companions

Examples of simple, commonly used alternating blocks are Snowball, Nine Patch, and Puss in the Corner. Some overall patterns, such as Irish Chain (see "Purple Passion" on page 27), use an A block that alternates with a B block to create a pleasing design. If you want to use an alternating block in an appliqué quilt, consider using a simple pieced or appliquéd design that relates to the primary block.

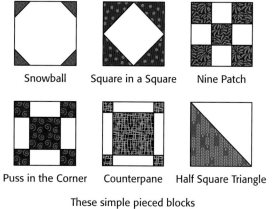

Snowball   Square in a Square   Nine Patch

Puss in the Corner   Counterpane   Half Square Triangle

These simple pieced blocks
can be used as alternating blocks.

Let's take a look at what happens when a Snowball block is used with a Nine Patch block. The squares at the corners of the Nine Patch and the triangles in the Snowball connect. In "Gabriel Meets Dick and Jane," the corners form a green diagonal flow in one direction and a blue diagonal flow in the other.

Alternating simple design blocks: "Gabriel Meets Dick and Jane" by Joan Hanson, 2000, Seattle, Washington, 47½" x 59½".

Compare "Batik Nine Patch" with "Gabriel Meets Dick and Jane." The same two blocks look completely different when the lights, mediums, and darks change places and the blocks are turned on-point.

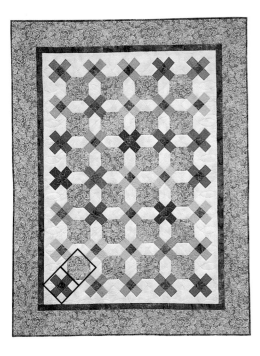

Alternating simple design blocks: "Batik Nine Patch" by Joan Hanson, 58" x 75". Quilted by Dawn Kelly.

With careful fabric selection, a Contrary Wife block and a Snowball block can connect to create a three-dimensional woven look.

Alternating simple design blocks: "Garden Path" by Joan Hanson, 41" x 41".

Alternating Big-Triangle Blocks

Big-triangle alternating blocks make it easy to cover a lot of ground, with dramatic results.

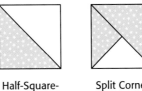

Half-Square-
Triangle Block

Split Corner
Triangle Block

To cut big half-square triangles, cut a square ⅞" larger than the finished block size. Cut the square in half diagonally to create two triangles. To make Split-Corner Triangle blocks, cut the large triangle as you would for a half-square triangle. For the two smaller triangles, cut a square that is 1¼" larger than the finished block size and cut the square in half twice on the diagonal to create four quarter-square triangles. Use two of these triangles in combination with the larger triangle to make a Split-Corner Triangle block.

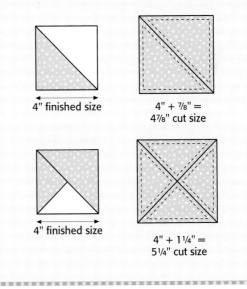

4" finished size

4" + ⅞" =
4⅞" cut size

4" finished size

4" + 1¼" =
5¼" cut size

Take a look at how three simple blocks result in dynamic quilts. "Scottish Chain" and "Chickens in the Chimney" are made from the same three blocks—Chimney Stone, Half-Square Triangle, and Split Corner Triangle—with "Scottish Chain" using a horizontal setting and "Chickens in the Chimney" using an on-point setting.

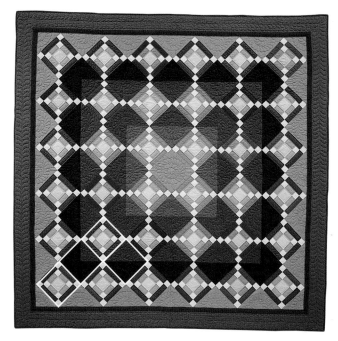

Alternating big-triangle blocks: "Chickens in the Chimney" by Mary Hickey, 1993, Seattle Washington, 88½" x 88½". Quilted by Sarah Hershberger.

"Permanent Incomplete" also uses big triangles in the alternating squares. When the triangles line up in one direction, they form diagonal rows.

Alternating big-triangle blocks: "Scottish Chain" by Joan Hanson, 1999, Seattle, Washington, 48½" x 48½".

Alternating big-triangle blocks: "The Permanent Incomplete" by Mary Hickey, 2000, Seattle Washington, 52" x 52". Machine quilted by Frankie Schmitt.

Alternating Three Blocks

Using three alternating blocks is a clever way to turn simple blocks into what might look like a complex quilt. "Breakfast in Bed" uses a plain square, a Rail Fence block, and a Nine Patch block, all set on point.

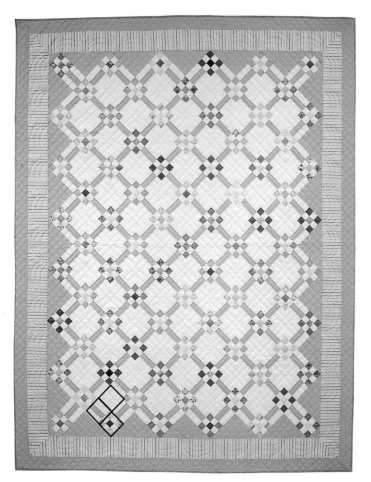

Alternating three blocks: "Breakfast in Bed" by Joan Hanson, 1993, Seattle, Washington, 88" x 113". Nine Patch blocks made by members of the Needle & I Guild, Seattle, Washington. Quilted by Polly Schlabach.

"Topsy Turvy Hearts" uses a plain square, a Square-in-a-Square block, and a Heart block, all set on point.

Alternating three blocks: "Topsy Turvy Hearts," designed and pieced by Mary Hickey, 33½" x 33½". Quilted by Frankie Schmitt.

"Cherry Star Picnic" uses a Star block, a Strip block, and an Hourglass block in a horizontal setting.

▶ Alternating three blocks: "Cherry Star Picnic," designed and pieced by Joan Hanson, 58½" x 58½". Quilted by Dawn Kelly.

Complex Companions

More elaborate blocks can also be used to create intricate overall designs. In "Kelley's Quilt," below left, careful placement of the light green fabric joins two blocks to form a diagonal tile effect, obscuring the boundaries of the blocks.

"Women in the Men's Club" below right, is another example of blocks whose boundaries blur to make one block appear larger than the other.

◀ Alternating complex design blocks: "Kelley's Quilt," designed and pieced by Joan Hanson, 56" x 72". Quilted by Dawn Kelly.

▶ Alternating complex design blocks: "Women in the Men's Club" by Joan Hanson and Mary Hickey, 1993, Seattle, Washington, 70½" x 70½". Quilted by Hazel Montague.

Stepping-Stone Blocks

Stepping-stone blocks connect with small squares, similar to stepping stones on a garden path. Nine Patch and Puss in the Corner blocks can be used as simple stepping-stone blocks. More complicated blocks can also be used. The one thing they all have in common is a link from corner to corner.

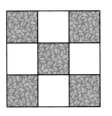
Simple Nine Patch

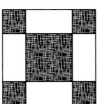
Puss in the Corner

Thrifty

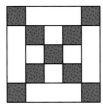
Country Lanes

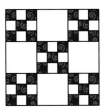
Double Nine Patch

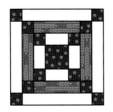
On the Square

Irish Chain designs alternate a stepping-stone block with another block to create a stair-step pattern. "Purple Passion" below right, is an example of a double Irish Chain with a soft color change.

The stepping-stone blocks in "Swedish Stepping Stars" below left, create a delicate diagonal path around the Star blocks.

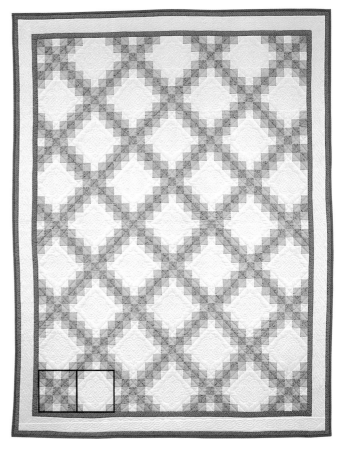

Alternating pieced stepping-stone blocks: "Purple Passion" by Joan Hanson, 1985, Seattle, Washington, 63" x 78". From the collection of Preston and Suzanne Martin.

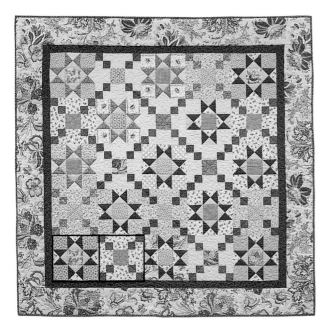

◀ Alternating pieced stepping-stone blocks: "Swedish Stepping Stars" by Mary Hickey, 2000, Seattle, Washington, 59" x 59". Machine quilted by Frankie Schmitt.

Pieced stepping-stone blocks can also partner with appliqué blocks. Since stepping-stone blocks are usually quicker to make than appliqué blocks, this setting can stretch a limited number of appliqué blocks into a relatively large quilt, as in "Happy Birthday Baby."

Five stepping-stone blocks and four embroidered blocks are used in "Redwork Airedales." The border completes the stepping-stone path.

Notice that "Tillie's Posy Pots" is set horizontally, and "It All Started with Ralph's Mother" is set on point.

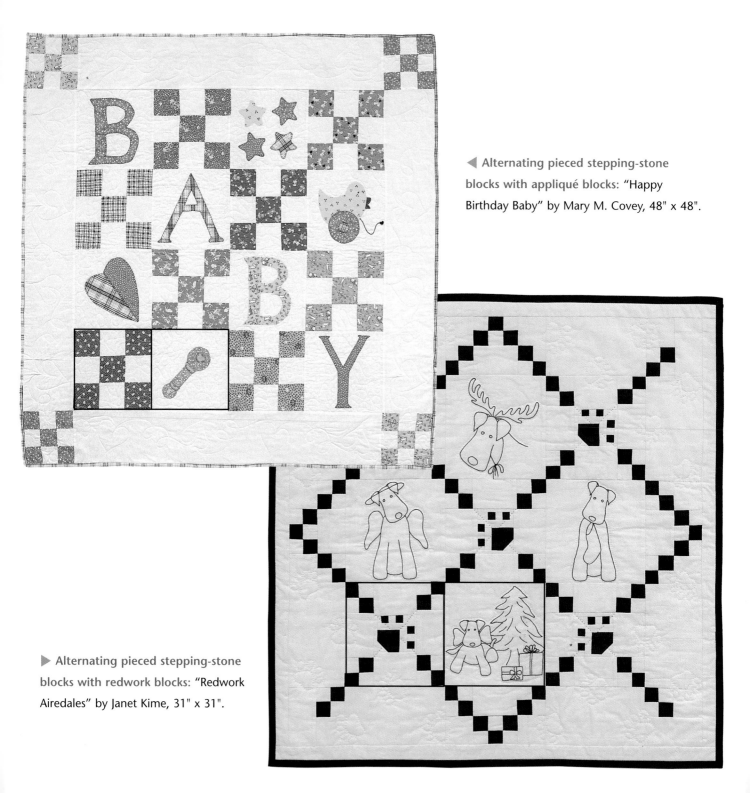

◀ Alternating pieced stepping-stone blocks with appliqué blocks: "Happy Birthday Baby" by Mary M. Covey, 48" x 48".

▶ Alternating pieced stepping-stone blocks with redwork blocks: "Redwork Airedales" by Janet Kime, 31" x 31".

Consider alternating design-block settings for:
- Irish Chain or other A block/B block designs
- Appliqué blocks
- Complex blocks that relate to a simple companion block

◀ Alternating pieced stepping-stone blocks with appliqué blocks: "Tillie's Posy Pots" by Joan Hanson, 1999, Seattle, Washington, 51" x 66".

▶ Alternating pieced stepping-stone blocks with appliqué blocks: "It All Started with Ralph's Mother" by Judy Pollard, 1993, Seattle, Washington, 67½" x 81¾". Quilted by Virginia Lauth.

Beyond the Blocks: Adding More Design Elements

DON'T THINK THAT JUST BECAUSE you've stitched a bunch of blocks you're ready to put your quilt top together. Adding sashing strips, setting squares, block frames, and other design elements can solve all sorts of problems. Sashing strips and setting squares can stretch a few blocks into a large quilt or allow you to combine complex blocks without matching every single seam from block to block. Framing strips allow you to even up inconsistently sized blocks or create a color theme where one is needed. Medallion settings make it easier to use a potentially awkward number of blocks successfully.

Simple Sashing

MANY BLOCKS LOOK BEST SET APART on their own, without the visual interference of neighboring blocks. Sampler blocks, for example, can be set with simple sashing between them to add a unifying element. This works especially well if the sashing fabric is a color that is contained within each of the blocks.

Experiment with sashing width—narrow sashing lets the design jump easily from block to block, as in "Christmas Bear Paw."

▶ Simple sashing: "Christmas Bear Paw" by Frieda Martinis, 1992, Everett, Washington, 70" x 82". Quilted by Frieda Martinis.

Matching Sashing

Using sashing that matches the background fabric used in the blocks makes the blocks appear to float on the surface of the quilt. In "Cabin in the Trees," the houses and trees are given enough room to stand on their own.

Contrasting Sashing

A contrasting sashing can highlight your blocks. The soft blue sashing in "Feedsack Flags" is light enough that it doesn't overpower the red and dark blue Flag blocks.

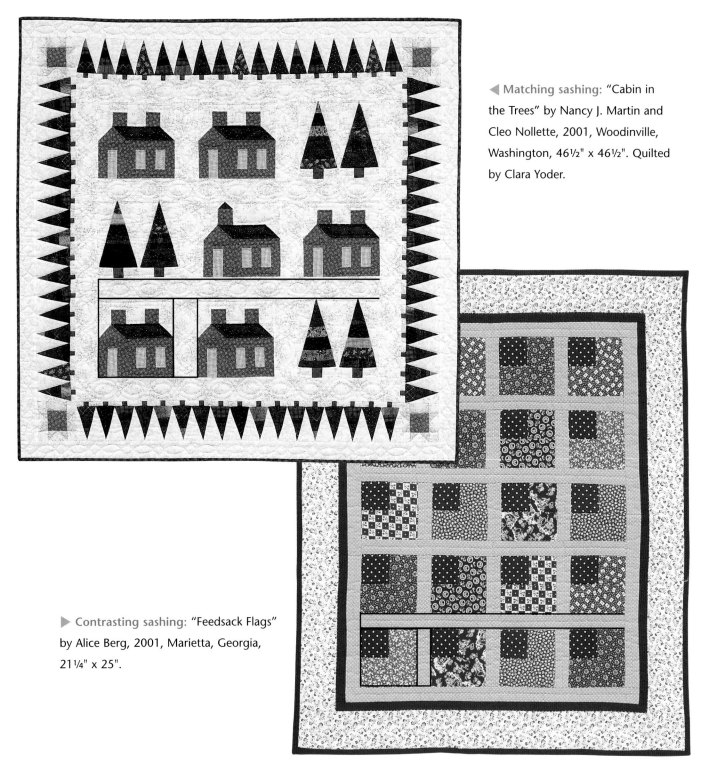

◄ Matching sashing: "Cabin in the Trees" by Nancy J. Martin and Cleo Nollette, 2001, Woodinville, Washington, 46½" x 46½". Quilted by Clara Yoder.

▶ Contrasting sashing: "Feedsack Flags" by Alice Berg, 2001, Marietta, Georgia, 21¼" x 25".

Floating Blocks with Sashing

"Big Dipper" features a dark sashing that blends with the setting triangles and border, so that the blocks seem to float.

Border Prints as Sashing

Border prints make wonderful sashing strips. "Christmas Bulbs" uses a wide floral print for the sashing, with vertical rows of blocks instead of the more usual horizontal rows.

Border prints as sashing: "Christmas Bulbs" by Nancy J. Martin, 2001, Woodinville, Washington, 53½" x 53½". Quilted by Frankie Schmitt.

Floating blocks with sashing: "Big Dipper" by Pat Speth, 1999, Davenport, Iowa, 81" x 106".

Consider a setting with simple sashing for:
- Sampler, Friendship, and scrappy blocks
- Visually dynamic blocks that stand on their own
- Picture blocks, such as House, Tree, and Basket blocks

CUTTING SASHING STRIPS

When cutting sashing pieces, cut the shorter strips the same length as the unfinished block. These short strips will fit between the blocks in each row. Choose a width that matches a patch size in the block, adding ½" for seam allowances. Cut the long sashing strips the same length as the rows. When you're assembling the rows and long sashing strips, make sure that the blocks and short sashing strips line up from row to row.

Sashing Strips and Setting Squares

ONCE YOU'VE COMPLETED A SET of blocks, adding sashing strips and setting squares may seem like too much trouble, but they can really enhance the look of your blocks. Think of sashing strips as long skinny blocks and setting squares as little blocks. Setting squares can be plain squares or pieced squares that repeat an element used in your blocks, such as a four-patch, nine-patch, or pinwheel unit.

Wide Sashing with Setting Squares

Wide sashing strips set blocks apart. Wide sashing can also stretch a limited number of blocks into a comparatively large quilt. Here the sashing pieces blend with the Arrows blocks, and the arrows point to appliqué hearts that float against the background.

Sashing with Contrasting Setting Squares

Sashing strips can match the block background, with a setting square punctuating the block intersections as in "Jelly Beans." Imagine what this quilt would look like without those scrappy little squares.

Sashing with contrasting setting squares: "Jelly Beans" by Sally Schneider, 2000, Breinigsville, Pennsylvania, 46" x 57".

◄ Wide sashing with setting squares: "Hearts and Arrows" by Joan Hanson, 1998, Seattle, Washington, 42" x 42".

Sashing That Forms Secondary Designs

The setting squares in "54-40 or Fight" and "Jewel Box" are the same size as the squares in the blocks, and they form a secondary nine-patch design at the corners of the blocks.

Sashing that forms secondary designs: "54-40 or Fight" by Nancy J. Martin, 2001, Woodinville, Washington, 60½" x 60½". Quilted by Mrs. Menno Miller.

Triangles at the ends of the sashing strips, which combine with the setting squares, add stars to "Dutch Treat Dishes." Notice how the star points continue in the yellow inner border to complete the outer row of stars.

Sashing that forms secondary designs: "Dutch Treat Dishes," designed and pieced by Joan Hanson, 66" x 78". Quilted by Dawn Kelly.

◀ Sashing that forms secondary designs: "Jewel Box" designed and pieced by Joan Hanson, 59½" x 74½". Quilted by Dawn Kelly.

Striped Sashing

Striped fabrics make wonderful sashing strips and borders. The multicolored stripe used as sashing in "Friendship Stars" unifies the different colors in the blocks.

Sashing in On-Point Settings

Who would want to try and sew these Wedding Ring blocks together side by side? Not I! With the sashing strips and setting squares arranged on-point, the blocks really sparkle. Notice how the setting squares along the edges turn into triangles. Another option would be to leave them as squares and make the side and corner setting triangles larger.

Sashing in on-point settings: "Honeymoon Suite" by Mimi Dietrich and Emily Watson, 2002, Baltimore, Maryland, 93" x 93".

◀ Striped sashing: "Friendship Stars" by Joan Hanson, 1999, Seattle, Washington, 45½" x 53".

Grouping Blocks with Sashing

Each village in "Country Village" consists of nine blocks sewn together, divided by sashing strips and setting squares.

Joining four or nine blocks with narrow sashing and then surrounding them with a wider sashing is another option. "Beary, Beary Strawberry" has four groups of four "paws."

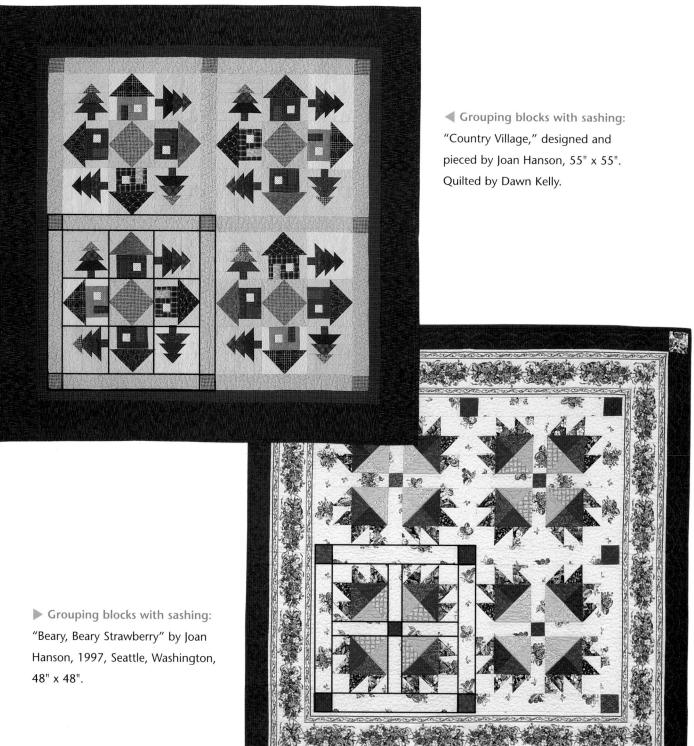

◄ Grouping blocks with sashing: "Country Village," designed and pieced by Joan Hanson, 55" x 55". Quilted by Dawn Kelly.

▶ Grouping blocks with sashing: "Beary, Beary Strawberry" by Joan Hanson, 1997, Seattle, Washington, 48" x 48".

Pieced Sashing

If you can't find just the right print for the sashing, try joining scrappy squares into sashing strips, as in "Hollyhock Wreath."

Pieced sashing increases your design options, allowing you to complete a design started in the blocks. Examine "Irish Trip" and notice how the narrow pieced sashing and setting squares continue the block pattern.

◀ Pieced sashing with plain setting squares: "Hollyhock Wreath" by Cleo Nollette, 1999, Seattle, Washington, 50½" x 50½".

▶ Pieced sashing with plain setting squares: "Irish Trip" by Elizabeth Hamby Carlson, 77" x 77". Quilted by Lizzie Borntrager.

The sashing used in "English Rose" and "Dorothy's Garden Girls" would be easy to strip piece using three fabric strips. "English Rose" uses strips that match the background of the blocks, so that the blocks and sashing strips blend together, while contrasting sashing strips set off the blocks in "Dorothy's Garden Girls." Pieced setting squares complete each design.

Consider a setting with sashing and setting squares for:
- Blocks that need a unifying element
- Quilts that you'd like to make bigger
- Blocks that create a secondary design when a setting square is added

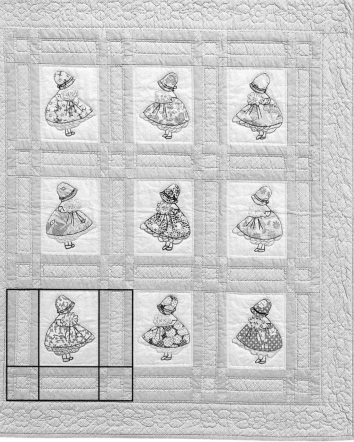

◀ Pieced sashing with pieced setting squares: "English Rose" by Joan Hanson, 36" x 48".

▶ Pieced sashing with pieced setting squares: "Dorothy's Garden Girls," blocks by Dorothy Everett Whitelaw, 1933. Assembled and quilted by Joan Hanson, 1989, Seattle, Washington, 43" x 47½".

Framed Blocks

FRAMING BLOCKS IS ONE OF my favorite setting options because it's a good way to standardize unevenly sized blocks that would otherwise be difficult to put together. This setting is great for Sampler and Friendship blocks, and for any other group of blocks that are not all the same size and/or shape.

To standardize blocks that are different sizes, add an oversized border or frame to each one, and then trim all the blocks to the same size. The strips that surround the blocks are known as "coping" strips, because they allow you to cope with unevenly sized blocks that would otherwise drive you crazy if you tried to piece them together. It may be necessary to vary the widths of the frames slightly, but the differences will be barely noticeable. The important thing is that you will ultimately have uniformly sized blocks that will be easy to put together. There are many frame variations from which to choose and endless ways to use them. Changing the color of the frame from block to block or changing the color from side to side on a block are among the many ways of setting such blocks together.

Straight-Cut Frames

The simplest frame is the straight-cut frame.

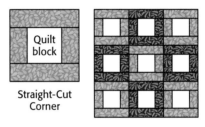

Straight-Cut
Corner

A narrow, straight-cut white frame surrounds the Heart blocks in "Little Sweethearts." Sashing and setting squares complete the design.

▶ Matching straight-cut frames: "Little Sweethearts" by Chris Mewhinney, 2000, Fairfield, Washington, 47" x 47".

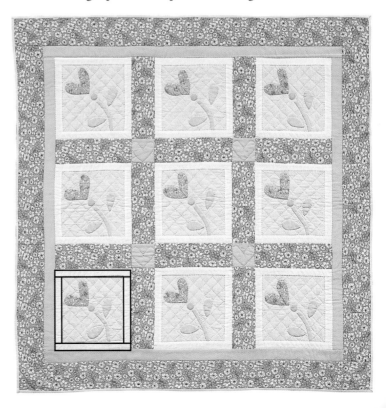

MAKING A STRAIGHT-CUT FRAME

1. Determine the finished width of the frame you want. Frames that are 1½" to 3" wide work well for most blocks. This is wide enough that any variation in the finished width of the frame won't be noticeable between blocks. Add 1" to 1½" to the finished width for seam allowances and a fudge factor. Since these frames will be trimmed down later, be kind to yourself and allow some extra fabric. Cut the length to match the unfinished size of your block. Stitch the frame to one side of your block and repeat for the opposite side.

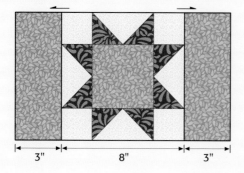

3"   8"   3"

2. Cut the strips for the top and bottom the same width as before. Determine the length of the strips by measuring the width of the block, including the side frames.

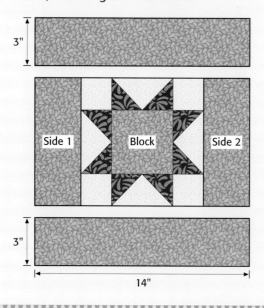

3"

Side 1   Block   Side 2

3"

14"

3. Attach the remaining two frames, just as if you were putting borders on a quilt.

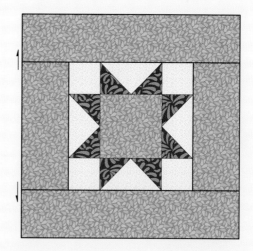

4. Determine a common size for the blocks and trim all of them to that size, keeping the design centered.

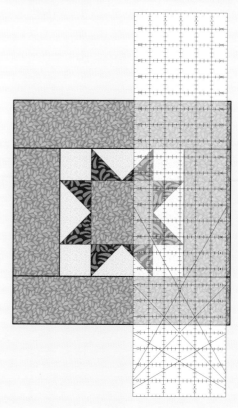

Use one fabric for half the frames and a contrasting fabric for the other half; then alternate colors when you put the blocks together. Or, use multiple colors for the frames for a scrappier look, as in "Framed Four Patch."

Two-Sided Frames

The "Sensational Settings Sampler Quilt" on page 56 features many framing techniques, including two-sided frames. To make a straight-cut, two-sided frame as shown, simply sew a strip to one side of the block and then add an adjacent strip.

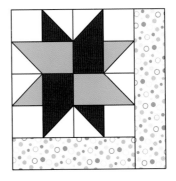

Mitered Frames

Frames with mitered corners are a bit trickier to sew, but they add depth. Try using the same fabric halfway around each block or on opposite sides, and then use another fabric to frame the other half. For a lovely 3-D effect, alternate blocks when you put them together.

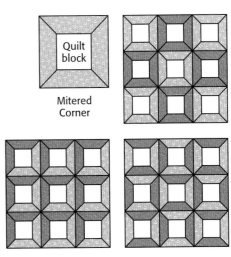

Scrappy straight-cut frames: "Framed Four Patch" by Virginia B. Kennedy, Jonesborough, Tennessee, 14" x 17½". Variation of "Framed Four Patch" from *Twenty Little Four-Patch Quilts* by Gwen Marston.

MITERING A FRAME CORNER

1. To determine the length of the frame strip, add the finished size of the block to twice the finished width of the frame strip. Add an inch or two to allow for easier handling. Cut four strips to this length.

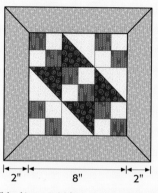

8" (block) + 4" (sides) + 2" (extra) = 14"

2. Using a sharp pencil, mark a dot on the wrong side of the block at the ¼" seam point at each corner.

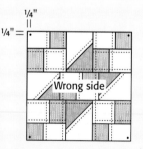

3. With right sides together, match the center of a frame strip to a center edge of the block. The strip will extend an equal distance beyond each end of the block. With the wrong side of the block facing up, sew the frame strip to the block, using a ¼"-wide seam allowance and starting and ending at the pencil dots. Backstitch at both ends. Repeat with the other three strips.

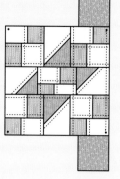

Stitch from dot to dot.

4. With right sides together, fold the block in half diagonally and arrange the frame strip on either side of the corner so that the long edges align as shown.

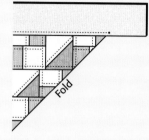

5. Using a ruler with a 45° angle line on it, align the 45° angle with the stitching line. Draw a line on the wrong side of each strip from the intersection of the stitching lines to the outer edge.

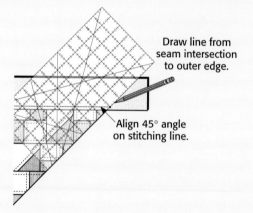

Draw line from seam intersection to outer edge.

Align 45° angle on stitching line.

6. Match and pin the drawn lines at the corner. Sew on the diagonal line, starting at the inside and backstitching at both ends. Repeat for each corner. Trim seams to ¼" and press open.

7. Trim all the blocks to a uniform size.

Attic Window Frames

Attic Window frames use strips on just two sides of the block, but two different colors are used and the corner is mitered. Careful placement of the light and dark colors create the illusion that light is shinning on the "window."

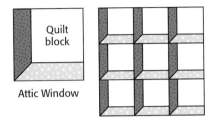

"The Incredibly Cool Cosmic Rocket Ship" places a dark blue sashing alongside the lighter blues of the Attic Window frames to inspire the feeling of looking at the night sky through a window.

Attic Window frames: "The Incredibly Cool Cosmic Rocket Ship" by Joan Hanson, 1993, Seattle, Washington, 67½" x 85". From the collection of Derek Hanson. Quilted by Laura Raber.

Tilted Frames

To add diagonal movement to your design, try tilted frames around your blocks.

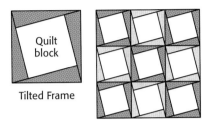

The Nine Patch blocks in "Dad's Quilt" are framed with a dark blue fabric, and the frames tip in alternating directions.

Tilted frames: "Dad's Quilt" by Robin Strobel, 1999, Issaquah, Washington, 54½" x 77". Quilted by Janice Nelson.

The Sailboat blocks in "Sunny Sailors" are surrounded with blue fabrics and set with an alternating plain block, while the blocks in "Tilted Pinwheels" are framed with different colors and set side by side to create a secondary pinwheel design. Tilted frames can tip in different directions, as in "Sunny Sailors," or in the same direction, as in "Tilted Pinwheels."

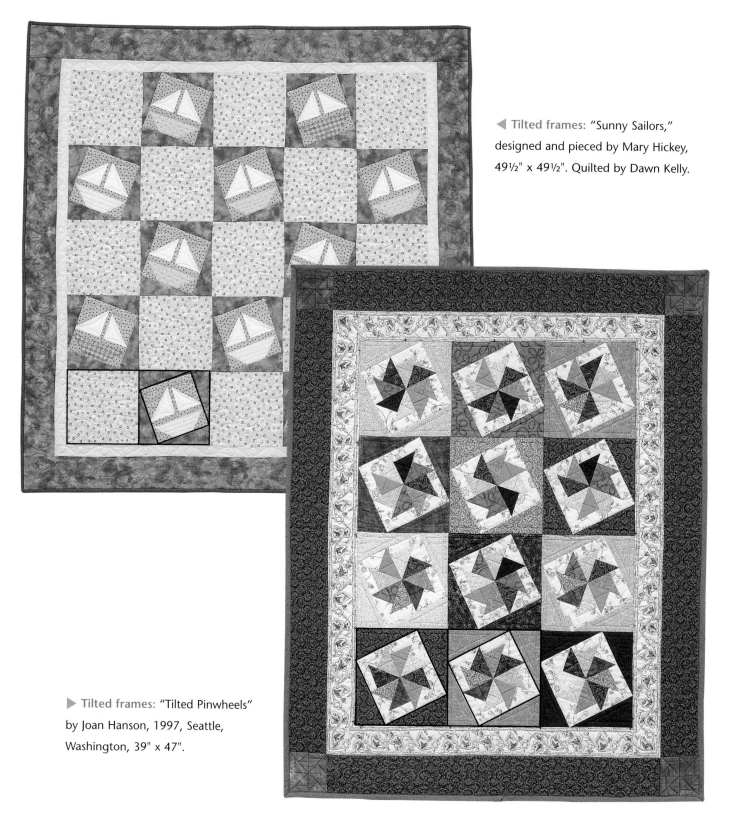

◄ Tilted frames: "Sunny Sailors," designed and pieced by Mary Hickey, 49½" x 49½". Quilted by Dawn Kelly.

▶ Tilted frames: "Tilted Pinwheels" by Joan Hanson, 1997, Seattle, Washington, 39" x 47".

CUTTING AND SEWING TILTED FRAMES

1. Determine the desired finished width of the frame, usually 1½" to 3" at its widest point. To the finished width, add 1" to 1½" for seam allowances and fudge factor. Since these frames will be trimmed down later, be kind to yourself and allow some extra fabric. Cut the length to match the *finished* size of your block plus the *cut* width of the frame. Cut four frames of this length.

2. Align a frame strip with the edge of the block. Stitch the strip to the block, leaving the last 1" open. Press the seam toward the frame.

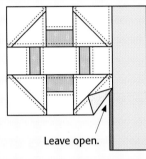

Leave open.

3. Sew a second frame strip to the adjacent, fully stitched edge. If you are using two or more fabrics, use a different fabric for the second strip.

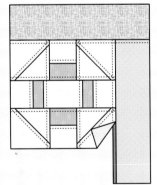

4. Choose a fabric for side three and sew as above. Repeat for side four.

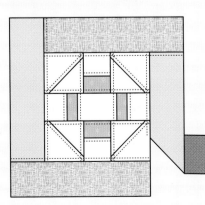

5. Complete the seam from side one by joining it to side four.

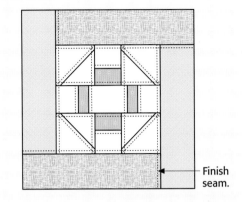

Finish seam.

6. Place a large square ruler (15") over the framed blocks at a pleasing angle, centering the block, and trim along the ruler's edge. If you don't have a square ruler large enough, use a 24"-long ruler.

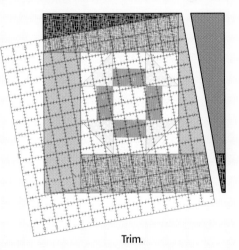

Trim.

NOTE: Blocks may be tilted in the opposite way by sewing and adding the frame strips in the opposite direction, and also trimming the frame in the opposite direction.

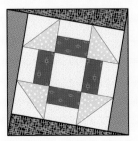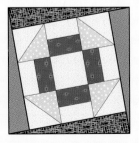

To carry this idea one step further, frame your blocks with multiple strips and then trim them to tilt as in "A Garden of Hearts."

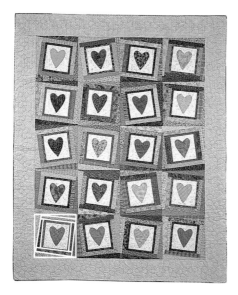

Tilted frames: "A Garden of Hearts" by Sandy Bonsib, 80½" x 96½".

Corner-Triangle Frames

To set a block on point, frame it with triangles.

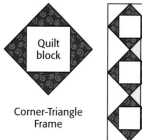

Corner-Triangle Frame

You can either cut triangles so that the block edges extend right to the seam line of the frame, or you can cut oversized triangles to "cope" with unevenly sized blocks and/or to float the blocks inside the triangle frame.

Frame fits block exactly.

Frame "floats" block.

Oversized triangles in alternating colors frame the Churn Dash blocks shown below.

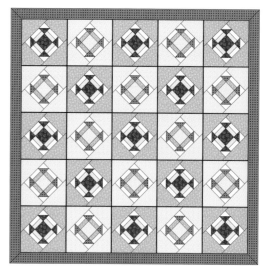

Floating blocks in triangle frames set side by side

Now let's take a look at them with sashing strips and setting squares included. Combining setting options creates many new design options.

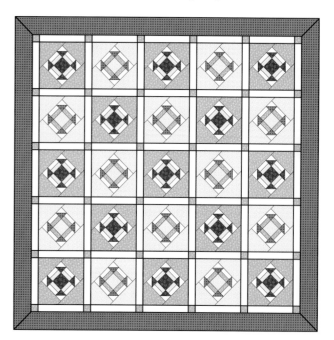

Floating blocks in triangle frames set side by side with sashing and setting squares

FLOATING BLOCKS IN TRIANGLE FRAMES

1. Referring to the chart on page 74, cut two squares for each block, adding 1" to 1½" to that measurement for a fudge factor. Cut the squares in half diagonally to make two triangles from each square.

2. Align the block edge with the center of the long side of the triangle, matching centers. Stitch, and repeat with the opposite side of the block. Press and trim seams toward the triangles.

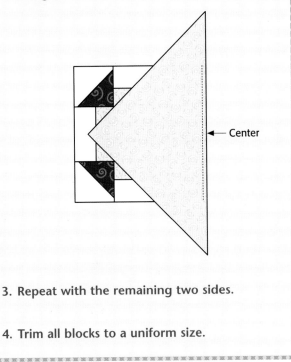

3. Repeat with the remaining two sides.

4. Trim all blocks to a uniform size.

Triangle frames can create a secondary star design when blocks are set side by side. "Flower Bed" uses alternating, scrappy green and pink frames to form a green star pattern. The border is pieced with green triangles to complete the design.

Triangle frames: "Flower Bed" by Jean Van Bockel, 2001, Coeur d'Alene, Idaho, 84" x 98".

Here, a Christmas print is framed twice with red and green triangles so that the center block is oriented correctly within the quilt. The reds and greens alternate position from block to block.

"Too Fruity" uses both straight and triangle frames. Notice how some of the blocks end up on-point while the rest stay horizontal. This setting would be a great way to combine on-point designs, such as Basket blocks, with horizontal blocks.

Double triangle frames: "Dick and Jane's Christmas Flannel Quilt" by Nancy J. Martin, Woodinville, Washington, 2001, 45" x 57". Quilted by Mattie Mast and Mary Mast.

Straight-cut and triangle frames: "Too Fruity" by Joan Hanson, 1992, Seattle, Washington, 58" x 75".

Consider a framed setting for:
- Sampler blocks
- Friendship blocks
- Blocks that aren't quite the same size
- On-point and horizontal blocks used in the same quilt

Strip Settings

IN A STRIP SETTING, blocks line up with each other in one direction, and they can be off-set or separated by sashing in the same direction or both horizontally and vertically.

Pictorial Quilts

If the sashing runs horizontally, it can create a landscape for houses, bunnies, cats, cars, trains, or other objects in your quilt. Your choice of sashing fabric can contribute to the illusion of a sidewalk, highway, train track, or grass strip, as in "Spring Flower Garden."

Or, the sashing can double as water, as in "Andrew and Patrick Sail Away."

Pictorial quilt in a strip setting: "Andrew and Patrick Sail Away" by Joan Hanson, 2000, Seattle, Washington, 31" x 40". From the collection of Andrew and Patrick Hanson.

◀ Pictorial quilt in a strip setting: "Spring Flower Garden," designed and pieced by Joan Hanson, 40" x 52". Quilted by Dawn Kelly.

Simple Vertical Rows

To create columns, run the blocks and sashing in vertical rows. The blocks in "Garland Star" are set on point, with side and corner triangles added to complete each vertical row. A large-scale floral print is used for the vertical sashing. Keep your eyes open for lovely, vine-type floral prints that could be used in a vertical sashing treatment.

"Kristen's Four Patch" uses simple Four Patch blocks, set on point with floral triangles, in vertical rows. Three fabric strips form the sashing.

◄ Simple vertical rows: "Garland Star" by Judy Pollard, 1990, Seattle, Washington, 81¼" x 94". Quilted by an unknown Amish quilter.

▶ Simple vertical rows: "Kristen's Four Patch" by Joan Hanson, 1996, Seattle, Washington, 32½" x 47". From the collection of Kristen Wrigley.

Offset Rows

On-point blocks set without sashing strips appear to float within the side and corner setting triangles. Dropping every other row by half a block creates a zigzag effect. To balance the quilt, use an odd number of rows. Offset rows are a good way to set a mathematically challenging number of blocks. For example, "Fantastic Fans and Beautiful Bows" uses 10 blocks, "Wiggle Flowers" uses 11 blocks, and "Little Shoo Fly" on page 52 uses 22 blocks.

◀ Offset rows: "Fantastic Fans and Beautiful Bows" by Joan Hanson, 1993, Seattle, Washington, 56" x 74". This quilt was inspired by Judy Pollard's Fantastic Fans quilt in *Tea Party Time* by Nancy J. Martin. Quilted by Mrs. John Burkholder.

▶ Offset rows: "Wiggle Flowers" by Mary Hickey, 32½" x 41". Quilted by Dawn Kelly.

Consider a strip setting for:

- Flying Geese blocks
- Pictorial blocks, such as trees, houses, bunnies, cats, cars, and trains
- A diagonal setting that would benefit from additional design movement
- A mathematically challenging number of blocks

Offset rows: "Little Shoo Fly" by Joan Hanson, 31¼" x 36¼".

Medallion Settings

THE MEDALLION SETTING CAN BE found in many variations, but there are basic guidelines you can use as a starting point: Medallions usually have one or more blocks as a central focus. From there, borders, blocks, or other elements are added. These elements might be pieced or appliquéd, or they could be a combination of both.

"Holly Berry Wreath" starts with a large pieced wreath in the center, with several "coping" border strips added to equal the width of the Bow Tie blocks used in the main border.

Medallion setting: "Holly Berry Wreath" by Joan Hanson, 53" x 53". Quilted by Dawn Kelly.

"Larkspur Farm Quilt" employs a combination of borders, including pieced and appliquéd, around a pictorial center block. A brown coping border frames the center block, expanding it to a size that will accommodate the pieced triangle border.

Medallion setting: "Larkspur Farm Quilt" by Jean Van Bockel, 2000, Coeur d'Alene, Idaho, 45" x 45".

COPING STRIPS

In a perfect world, checkbooks would always balance and quilt blocks would always turn out to be the size we intend them to be. Since this isn't a perfect world, we need ways of making do with what we have. Use coping strips to even up sections of quilts that aren't quite the right size. For example, coping strips come in handy when blocks are unevenly sized, especially when the blocks are set on point and corner triangles are involved. Cut coping strips wider than you need, sew them to the block or quilt section, and then trim the entire block or section to a standard size.

Quilt elements can switch from a diagonal setting to a horizontal setting. Consider this option when you want to use a large central block or group of blocks in combination with blocks in a border. "Line Dancing Lilies" uses four blocks in the center, several coping strips around the central blocks to accommodate an inner checkerboard border, and corner triangles that turn the entire center section on point. Corner triangles turn the border blocks, three on top and three on bottom, on point as well. The block borders change the shape of the quilt from a square to a rectangle. This is a clever way to use ten blocks in a quilt.

Medallion setting: "Line Dancing Lilies" by Mary Hickey, 1993, Seattle, Washington, 86" x 102⅝". Quilted by Susie Eerb.

DESIGNING ON GRAPH PAPER

If you're planning a quilt on graph paper and you want to switch from a diagonal to a horizontal orientation, it may be helpful to first draft and cut out your center design and then paste it onto a new sheet of graph paper. This way, when you change to the other orientation, your graph grid will accommodate the direction of your design. For example, if the center blocks are set diagonally with corner triangles and other blocks are set horizontally, place your graph paper sections so that they are oriented in the same direction as the blocks, diagonally and horizontally.

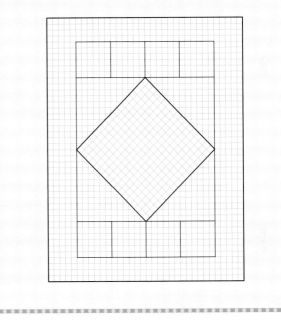

Consider a medallion setting for:
- A single central block or a large central block used in combination with smaller blocks
- A group of blocks that creates a focal point
- Blocks that are different sizes

Sensational Settings Sampler Quilt

By Joan Hanson, 66½" x 87½", 2003. There are 22 blocks,
each measuring 8" finished. Quilted by Dawn Kelly.

NOW THAT YOU'VE SEEN VARIOUS categories of setting options, consider combining more than one in the same quilt. Take a look at the "Settings Sampler" quilt and see how many setting options come together in this one design.

- The center consists of four blocks set side by side.
- Four types of frames are used: straight-cut, corner triangle, two-sided, and tilted.
- The framed blocks create a medallion star.
- Some blocks are set horizontally and some on-point.
- Tilted-frame blocks form top and bottom borders.
- A coping-strip border adds width to the center, accommodating the length of the tilted-frame border.
- In all, 22 blocks are used.

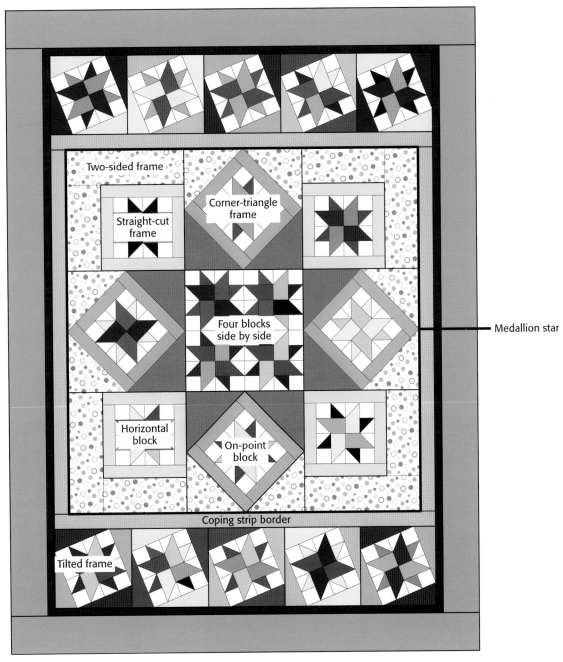

22-Block Setting

SETTING OPTIONS

Scrappy, 8" Spinning Star blocks were used throughout the sample quilt, but any blocks of equal size would work. In fact, this setting is ideal for using horizontal and on-point blocks in the same quilt. Choose four blocks that measure 8" square when finished and place them in the middle of the quilt. The remaining blocks will be framed, and the frames trimmed to a consistent size.

This setting uses 22 blocks, but it will work for 12 blocks if you eliminate the top and bottom tilted-frame borders. Or, by placing blocks on all four sides, you could add 14 more blocks—7 on each side—for a total of 36. Or, by adding a block at each corner of the outer border (increasing the border size to 8"), you could add another 4 blocks to any of the above options.

12-Block Setting

16-Block Setting

36-Block Setting

MATERIALS

All yardages are based on 42"-wide fabric.

1½ yards total of assorted background fabrics for blocks

1½ yards of medium blue for outer border

1⅛ yards of periwinkle blue for the large star points and binding

1 yard of multicolored, large-dot print for the background of the center medallion

½ yard *each* of light and dark values of blue, pink, green, and yellow for Star blocks and tilted frames (8 fabrics total)

½ yard of medium pink for the framed blocks

½ yard of pale green for the framed blocks

½ yard of medium green for the inner border

½ yard of bright pink for the middle border

5½ yards for the backing (2 widths pieced vertically)

72" x 93" piece of batting

CUTTING

From the assorted background fabrics for blocks, cut:

    12 squares for each block, 2½" x 2½", for a total of 264

From the light and dark star fabrics, cut:

    4 squares for each block, 2½" x 2½", for a total of 88

    4 rectangles for each block, 2½" x 4½", for a total of 88

From *each* of the light and dark star fabrics, cut:

    2 strips, 3" x 42", for a total of 16 strips; crosscut each strip into 3 rectangles, 3" x 12"

From the medium pink for the framed blocks, cut:

    5 strips, 2⅛" x 42"; crosscut into eight 2⅛" x 8½" rectangles and eight 2⅛" x 11¾" rectangles

From the pale green for the framed blocks, cut:

    5 strips, 2⅛" x 42"; crosscut into eight 2⅛" x 8½" rectangles and eight 2⅛" x 11¾" rectangles

From the periwinkle blue, cut:

    4 squares, 8⅞" x 8⅞"; cut each square in half once diagonally to yield 8 half-square triangles

    9 strips, 2½" x 42"

From the multicolored, large-dot print, cut:

    4 squares, 8⅞" x 8⅞"; cut each square in half once diagonally to yield 8 half-square triangles

    4 strips, 5¼" x 42"; crosscut into four 5¼" x 11¾" rectangles and four 5¼" x 16½" rectangles

From the bright pink, cut:

    8 strips, 1¾" x 42"

From the medium blue, cut:

    8 strips, 6" x 42"

PIECING THE SPINNING STAR BLOCKS

Refer to the quilt photo for fabric-placement ideas.

1. With right sides together, place a 2½" background square on a 2½" star-fabric square. Draw a diagonal pencil line on the background square as shown. Sew on the line. Cut ¼" from the sewn line. Press the seam toward the star-fabric triangle. Repeat to make 4 half-square triangle star-point units.

Make 2 light and 2 dark.

2. With right sides together, align a 2½" background square with one end of a 4½" star-fabric rectangle. Draw a diagonal pencil line on the background square as shown. Sew on the line. Cut ¼" from the sewn line. Press the seam

toward the star rectangle. Repeat to make 4 rectangular star-point units.

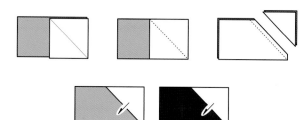

Make 2 light and 2 dark.

3. With right sides together, sew a 2½" background square to a unit from step 1. Press the seam toward the background square. Repeat to make 4 units.

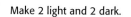

Make 4.

4. With right sides together, sew a unit from step 3 to a rectangular star-point unit. Press toward the star-point unit. Repeat to make 4 quarter-star units.

Make 4.

5. With right sides together, sew 2 quarter-star units together. Repeat to make 2 half-star units. Press the seams as shown.

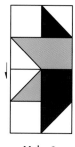

Make 2.

6. With right sides together, join the half-star units to complete the block. Press the final seam to one side.

PIECING THE CENTER MEDALLION

1. With right sides together, join two Spinning Star blocks and press the seam to one side. Repeat for the remaining two blocks, pressing the seam in the opposite direction. Sew the block pairs together and press the seam allowance to one side.

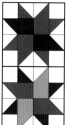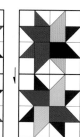

2. Choose blocks to go around the center section, four to be diagonally set and four to be horizontally set. Use the medium pink 2⅛" rectangles to frame the on-point blocks and pale green 2⅛" rectangles to frame the horizontal blocks.

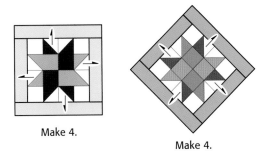

Make 4.

Make 4.

3. Sew periwinkle triangles to two adjacent sides of each pink-framed block and multicolored dot triangles to the remaining two sides as shown. Press the seams toward the triangle frames.

Make 4.

4. Sew a 5¼" x 11¾" multicolored dot rectangle to one side of each horizontal block. Press the seam toward the multicolored rectangle. Sew a 5¼" x 16½" multicolored rectangle to the adjacent side as shown. Press the seam toward the multicolored rectangle.

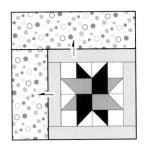

Make 4.

5. Join the blocks into rows, pressing as shown. Join the rows and press the final seams to one side.

PIECING THE TILTED-FRAME BLOCKS

1. From the 3" x 12" star-fabric rectangles, choose two dark and two light rectangles to frame each block. Referring to "Cutting and Sewing Tilted Frames" on page 45, sew the rectangles to the blocks, being careful to place dark rectangles on opposite sides and light rectangles on opposite sides.

2. Using a large, square ruler, center and tilt the framed block to a pleasing angle and trim to an 11" square.

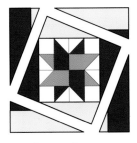

Trim to 11" square.

3. Butting the dark and light frames against each other, join five blocks to make the top row of blocks and the remaining five blocks to make the bottom row. Press the seams to one side.

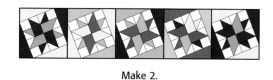

Make 2.

ASSEMBLING THE QUILT

1. Measure the center medallion. It should be 48½" square, including seam allowances. Measure the tilted-block rows. They should be 53" long, including seam allowances. Take the difference between your actual measurements, divide by two, and add ½" for seam allowances. (If your cutting and stitching was mathematically precise, you'll come up with 2¾" for this measurement.) You'll use the resulting number as the width of the green inner border strips. This border is a coping strip and, like the frames around unevenly sized blocks, it helps everything fit together nicely.

2. From the medium green, cut 6 strips across the width of the fabric, using the measurement you arrived at in step 1 for the strip width. Cut two of the medium green strips in half. Sew one of these half-strips to the end of each of the remaining strips. Press the seam allowance open. Sew a pieced strip to each side of the center section. Trim the ends even and press the seam toward the border. Repeat for the top and bottom of the center section, using the remaining border strips.

53" (tilted block row) – 48½" (center medallion) = 4½"
4½" ÷ 2 (side borders) = 2¼" (border width)
2¼" + ½" (seam allowance) = 2¾" (border strips)

3. Sew the tilted-block rows to the top and bottom. Press the seams toward the border strip.

4. Sew the bright pink strips together in pairs to make four long inner-border strips. Sew two strips to the sides of the quilt. Trim the ends even and press the seam allowances toward the border. Repeat for the top and bottom of the quilt, using the remaining border strips. Press.

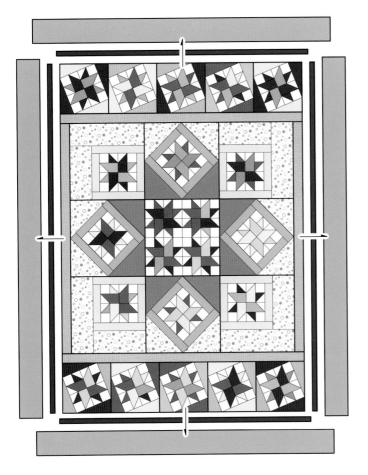

5. Repeat step 3 with the medium blue strips.

FINISHING THE QUILT

1. After removing selvages along seam edges, piece the quilt backing together. Press the seams open. Layer the backing, batting, and quilt top and baste the layers together.

2. Quilt as desired. This quilt was machine quilted.

3. Trim the excess batting and backing from the quilt edges and square up the quilt top.

4. Prepare and attach the binding, using the 2½" periwinkle blue strips. For detailed instructions on the binding process, I recommend Mimi Dietrich's *Happy Endings* (Martingale & Company, 2003).

Designing Your Quilt

NOW IT'S TIME TO GATHER ALL YOUR IDEAS and inspirations and start working on a quilt plan. For some quilts, a simple paper napkin sketch will do. Others might require an elaborate scale drawing on graph paper, complete with color placement, or a computer illustration with actual fabrics scanned in. A detailed approach can help you determine how much of each fabric you'll need and exactly where each block will go. Or you might prefer to improvise as you go. Choose the approach that works for your project and for you.

EQUIPMENT

As with any task, gathering necessary supplies and working in a suitable space with adequate lighting makes the job go more smoothly. Try to find a table or desk where you can leave your work in progress (also known as mess!) and come back to it whenever you have a few minutes or when a new idea comes to mind. You'll get a lot more done and use smaller bits of time if you don't have to get everything out each time you want to work and then put everything away when you're finished.

DESIGNING WITH BLOCKS

If you're starting with a stack of blocks, you'll want to know how many you have, what their *finished* sizes are, and how true to size each block is. If your blocks vary more than ¼" in size, you may want to design a setting in which the blocks do not meet side by side.

Books, magazines, photos, quilt sketches: You'll find many examples of setting possibilities in the pages of this book, but keep your eyes open for quilts that are set in other ways as well. Take your camera or a pad of paper to quilt shows and guild meetings to record settings that you like. When you're looking through quilt books or magazines, tab pages that have appealing settings, using sticky notes or markers, so that you can find them easily later.

Calculator: Since quiltmaking does involve some math, a calculator is helpful. Because a calculator gives you decimals and we're used to working in inches and fractions of inches in quiltmaking, you'll find the conversion chart on page 73 helpful.

Flannel board or design wall: Placing your blocks on a flannel board or even on a piece of batting tacked to the wall (or to a piece of foam-core board) allows you to stand back and squint at your blocks to audition different arrangements, fabrics, borders, and sashing treatments. What looks wonderful on paper might not look so wonderful in real life, so this is a good way to test your ideas.

Reducing glass: A reducing glass looks like a magnifying glass, but it has a concave lens that reduces what you are looking at. Reducing glasses come in handy when you're using a design wall and want to see how your blocks will look from a distance.

DESIGNING ON PAPER

If you're drafting on paper, you'll want the following tools.

Graph paper: You'll find graph paper in notebook-size tablets and in large single sheets (usually 17" x 22"). The smaller size is handy to carry with you for sketching, and the larger sheets work well for planning complex projects at home. The most common scale of graph paper is four squares to the inch, but it's also available in five, six, and eight squares to the inch. These additional scales come in handy when you're working with blocks based on a specific grid and you want to draft the blocks to scale. If you're working with blocks based on a nine-patch grid, use graph paper with six squares to the inch so that the divisions in the block match up with the lines on the graph—two squares per division. When I'm working with a stack of blocks, I usually use a 1" or ½" square to represent the block and then work out the size from there.

Tracing paper: Rather than drafting a quilt setting directly on graph paper, you might sometimes want to place tracing paper on top of graph paper to make your sketch. This method not only saves graph paper but also eliminates all the extra lines on the graph paper from interfering with the quilt design. It also makes it easier to include both horizontal and diagonal design elements in your sketch, because you can change the orientation of the graph paper under the tracing paper. Tracing paper works especially well when you're planning a medallion-style setting in which the orientation of the blocks might change from horizontal to diagonal and back again.

Narrow acrylic ruler: A 2" x 18" thin, clear acrylic ruler is useful for drafting designs and making templates. These rulers are marked in inches with ⅛" divisions. They're not made to be used with a rotary cutter, as they are so thin that the cutting

blade will roll onto the top of the ruler and ruin the edge. The 1" x 6" and 1" x 12" sizes are handy for drafting smaller shapes.

Drawing pencils: Mechanical pencils are preferable because they consistently produce a sharp, fine line, but any sharp pencil will work. Be sure to keep a good supply on hand.

Erasers: A big, white artist's eraser is to sketching what the seam ripper is to sewing. Don't be without one!

Removable tape and/or glue stick: Removable tape or liquid glue will do for pasting graph-paper designs together, but glue sticks are easy to use. Look for the sticks made of repositionable glue, the ones that allow you to adhere a piece and then move it.

Paper scissors: Use paper scissors when cutting and pasting graph-paper designs together. Don't use your good fabric scissors!

Colored pencils or markers: When designing on graph paper, I use colored pencils to shade in my sketched design. I like a wide assortment of colors, either pencils or markers, but I find it's easier to get light and dark color variations when using pencils.

Mirrors: Two 12"-square mirrors, or smaller mirrors often available at quilt shops, will come in handy. Placed at right angles, they can give you an idea of what your blocks will look like repeated over and over again. Place the mirrors at adjacent edges of your design and see what happens. It's magic!

Fresnel viewing lenses: Looking at a block through a Fresnel viewing lens, available at some quilt shops, repeats it over and over to give you a sense of what it would look like repeated.

The Design Process

Step 1: By now, you have some idea of settings that you like. Your first sketches will probably be quite crude. Don't worry about using a ruler at this point. The main thing is to get your ideas down on paper—any kind of paper—before you forget them. At this point, you're just making outlines of block settings—you're not sketching particular block designs. I like starting out with the "paper-napkin approach," to get the creativity flowing, putting down several possibilities that seem to have merit. Don't worry about being neat and tidy or coloring in your design. That can come later in the fine-tuning stage.

Start with simple setting outlines.

Step 2: Before going any further, you may want to sketch designs for the block(s) you'll use. If you are working with a pieced block, use graph paper in whichever scale matches your block. If you are making a large quilt with lots of repeating blocks, sketch your block so that 1½" is equal to one block. That way, graph paper that is divided into ⅛" squares will match up with a variety of block grids (including nine-patch and sixteen-patch). If you're working with a complex block, a large block, or an assortment of different blocks, use two or three inches to equal one block. The scale is really up to you and how big you want your working drawing to be.

Make enough copies of your block so that you can cut them out and arrange, and rearrange, them into various designs.

Experiment with different block arrangements.

Step 3: Place a piece of tracing paper over your graph paper, orienting the graph paper for a horizontal or diagonal grid as desired. A few small pieces of removable tape will hold the tracing paper in place. If you are planning a medallion-style setting in which the block orientation changes, start with the center orientation and then reposition your tracing paper as you go along. Using an acrylic ruler and a sharp pencil, sketch out your setting design, leaving blank spaces so that you can tape or glue copies of your blocks in place. This is the point where you can audition various options, such as different alternating blocks, framing ideas, or different sashing widths. If your quilt needs to be a predetermined size for a certain wall space or bed, adjust the width of the sashing strips, frames, borders, and other components so that your quilt will be the required size. (For more information on bed sizes, see page

73.) To speed up the process, you can assemble just a portion of the quilt setting and then use two mirrors or a Fresnell viewing lens to see how your design will look when repeated.

Set up a pair of mirrors to see what a block would look like if set side by side with identical blocks.

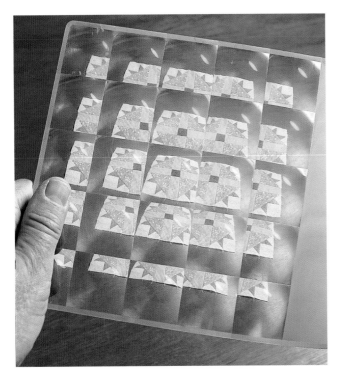

Use a Fresnel viewing lens to get a less precise image of possible repeat designs.

Step 4: When you are pleased with your design, tape or glue the various paper pieces in place. Make several copies of your finished design. Get out your colored pencils or markers and color the design in various ways. Keep in mind that light colors come forward while dark colors tend to recede. If you want to use a strong color, try using it in small amounts so that it won't overpower other parts of your design. This is your opportunity to try changing colors from the center to the edges of your design or to try "floating" the blocks with sashing or alternating blocks. Don't forget that each setting you design could work well in a number of color schemes. Finalize your setting design and color scheme.

Color your chosen block arrangement.

Step 5: Using the size of your block as a guide, determine the size of the other parts of your setting. Make an inventory list of component parts that you'll need to complete your top. Decide which fabrics will be used for each component of your design. This fabric list can be as detailed or as sketchy as you wish. By now, you'll have a good idea of the size of your quilt, so you should be able to determine how much fabric you'll need for the binding and backing and what size batting you'll need.

Step 6: Once you've decided which parts of your quilt will be cut from which fabric, estimate your fabric needs for blocks, setting triangles, sashing strips, and so on. When I purchase fabric, I usually buy from ½ to 1 yard extra to allow for mistakes and to provide insurance in case I change color placements along the way.

Step 7: Collect fabrics from your stash and go shopping for more fabric!

USING QUILT-DESIGN SOFTWARE

Why design on a computer? To play with block design, color placement, and sashing and border options; to print perfectly sized patterns; to rotate blocks and discover new secondary designs; or even to resize blocks and turn a twin-size quilt into a baby quilt—or into a king-size quilt—in seconds. All before you ever cut a piece of fabric. Many wonderful possibilities await you when you use quilting software.

Quiltmaking software, such as Quilt-Pro and Electric Quilt, offers all sorts of design opportunities. Compare different software packages to find the one that suits you best. If you're unsure what to buy, ask your quilting friends about their experiences, check reviews online, and ask for advice at your local quilt shop. Many quilt shops sell quiltmaking software and allow you to try it out right there in the store.

Although software packages differ, and regular upgrades are sure to alter the available features, chances are you'll want to experiment with the following building blocks of patchwork.

Designing the Blocks

Depending on the software you use, you might have the ability to draw blocks using a variety of grid options and/or the option to choose from thousands of ready-made blocks. On your computer, you can change block sizes, print copies for foundation piecing, and color the design as many ways as you like.

Creating the Layout

Experiment with horizontal versus diagonal settings, number of rows, number of blocks in each row, and block size. Play with sashing styles and widths, and then move on to borders. How many and what type you want (mitered, simple straight-cut, straight-cut with cornerstones, pieced borders, and so on). After deciding how many and what type of border, try out different border widths to see what you like.

Setting the Blocks

You've chosen a setting layout, and now you can try different block placements. Once your blocks are in place, if your software supports such a function, you might want to flip and rotate them to see what secondary designs might emerge. This is especially fun with asymmetrical blocks such as Log Cabin.

Coloring the Quilt

Your quilt really comes to life as you start to experiment with color options. You can use an endless palette of solid colors and even scans, which might be included in your software, of actual quilting fabrics. Or you can scan fabrics from your own collection. What would your blocks look like with dark blue sashing and red setting squares? Or how about off-white sashing and light blue setting squares? With just a few keystrokes you can find out and save each design option to consider later. Changing the block and border colors is just as easy. You might even be able to add appliqué designs and quilting patterns to your project.

Quilt 1   Quilt 2   Quilt 3

Quilt 4   Quilt 5   Quilt 6

Final Quilt Colorations

Figuring Yardage Requirements

Designing quilts on a computer is so much fun that it's easy to forget the real goal is to actually make a quilt out of fabric. But how much fabric will you need? Quilt-design software can provide yardage estimates for all of your fabrics.

Printing the Quilt

Printing a line drawing or colored drawing of your quilt (on a color printer) is easy and provides a great sewing guide. You might even want to email your "paper quilts" to your on-line quilt buddies. Now gather fabric and start sewing the real thing!

Special Considerations

LET'S TAKE A LOOK AT SEVERAL common problems you may run into when working with actual blocks, such as setting blocks that aren't quite the same size, or setting unusual numbers of blocks together.

HANDLING BLOCKS THAT AREN'T QUITE THE SAME SIZE

Sometimes, no matter how hard you try, blocks just don't end up all the same size. This often happens when Sampler and Friendship blocks are made by lots of different people. When your blocks are different sizes, first square them up with a 12" or 15" square acrylic ruler and a rotary cutter. Trim off the uneven parts along each side and try to end with all the blocks as close to the same size as possible.

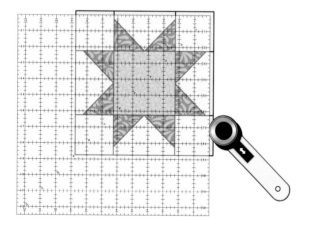

If the difference in sizes ranges from no more than ⅛" to ¼", you'll probably be able to join your blocks using the fudge-to-fit method. If the difference is greater, you may need to frame the blocks to standardize the size. If some of your blocks are one size and all the rest are a different size, you might want to try a medallion setting.

Fudge to Fit

When the difference in block sizes falls into the ⅛" to ¼" range, join them with the fudge-to-fit method.

As you piece blocks, place the smaller of the two blocks on top, with right sides together. Pin the ends and any intersecting seams and points that need to match. If seams don't quite match up, you may need to decide which are going to show the most and match those, settling for "just close" on the others.

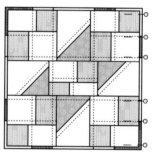

Place the smaller block on top and match seams.

As you stitch the blocks together, the feed dog on your sewing machine will pull more on the larger block, helping to ease the excess into the seam. You may need to hold on to both ends of your blocks and pull gently to stretch them as you stitch.

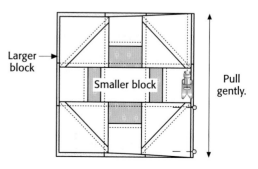

Larger block

Smaller block

Pull gently.

Frame to Fit

If your block sizes vary too much for fudging, you might want to standardize them with frames. Review the framing options and methods in "Framed Blocks" on pages 39–48 and choose one or more that are suited to your blocks.

The Medallion Connection

If most of your blocks are the same size, with only a few oddballs to worry about, consider a medallion setting like the one used for the "Sensational Settings Sampler Quilt" on page 56. Stitch together the four blocks that are closest in size for the center medallion. Hopefully, the remaining blocks will be fairly close in size. If not, you might want to add setting triangles or framing strips. For more information on medallion options, refer to "Medallion Settings" on pages 53–55.

SETTING AN UNUSUAL NUMBER OF BLOCKS

It's a snap to figure how to set thirty blocks together. You can easily set them in six rows with five blocks in each row, but what do you do with twenty-six blocks? Thirteen rows of two blocks in each row isn't practical. An odd number of blocks, such as seven or seventeen, presents the same kind of challenge. There are several solutions to consider when the number of blocks that you want to use doesn't divide evenly into rows.

Alternating Blocks

When a main block alternates with another block, the blocks are usually arranged so that an odd number of blocks is used in each row, with an odd number of rows in the quilt so that the same block will end up in each corner. If you multiply the odd number of blocks in a row by the odd number of rows, you'll end up with an odd number of total blocks needed. If you divide the total number of blocks needed into two groups, one group will have one more block than the other.

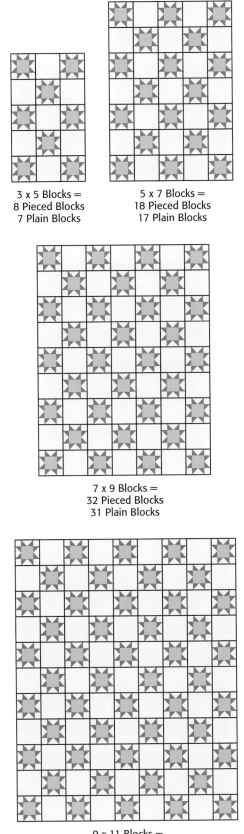

3 x 5 Blocks =
8 Pieced Blocks
7 Plain Blocks

5 x 7 Blocks =
18 Pieced Blocks
17 Plain Blocks

7 x 9 Blocks =
32 Pieced Blocks
31 Plain Blocks

9 x 11 Blocks =
50 Pieced Blocks
49 Plain Blocks

Using Diagonal Settings

Diagonal settings, in which primary blocks are set side by side or alternated with secondary blocks, can also accommodate an odd number of blocks. If your initial blocks are oriented horizontally, add corner-triangle framing to change them to a diagonal orientation.

Creating Medallions

A medallion setting might be the answer for a challenging number of blocks. Take another look at the medallion settings on pages 53–55 and the number of blocks in each.

Don't Forget the Border

If you have four blocks too many, make a border that's the same width as your blocks and put one block in each corner. If you still have one block left over, incorporate it into your label on the back of the quilt.

5 Blocks

7 Blocks

8 Blocks

9, 11, or 13 Blocks

14 or 18 Blocks

17 or 22 Blocks

26, 28, or 32 Blocks

31 Blocks

Quick Reference Charts

THIS SECTION CONTAINS CHARTS AND other reference materials to help simplify many of the common calculations you need to make when designing a quilt.

COMMON BED SIZES

If you're designing a quilt for a specific bed, it's best to measure the actual bed. If that isn't possible, use the chart below.

BED	MATTRESS SIZE
Crib	23" x 46"
Youth	32" x 66"
Twin	39" x 75"
Double	54" x 75"
Queen	60" x 80"
King	78" x 80"
California King	72" x 84"

DECIMAL TO INCH CONVERSIONS

When you're using a calculator, you'll have to work with decimals. Use this chart to convert decimals to fractions or to round decimal measurements off to the nearest 1/8".

DECIMAL		FRACTION
.125	=	1/8"
.25	=	1/4"
.375	=	3/8"
.50	=	1/2"
.625	=	5/8"
.75	=	3/4"
.875	=	7/8"
1.0	=	1"

DIAGONAL MEASUREMENTS OF STANDARD-SIZE BLOCKS

When you set blocks diagonally, it's helpful to know the diagonal measurement of the block so that you can determine the quilt size. To figure the diagonal block size, multiply the finished length of one side of the block by 1.414, or use the chart below.

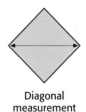

Diagonal measurement

BLOCK SIZE	DIAGONAL MEASUREMENT
2"	2⅞"
3"	4¼"
4"	5⅝"
5"	7⅛"
6"	8½"
7"	9⅞"
8"	11¼"
9"	12¾"
10"	14⅛"
12"	17"
14"	19⅞"
16"	22⅝"
18"	25½"
20"	28¼"
24"	34"

CALCULATING CORNER AND SIDE TRIANGLES

It's important to cut corner and side triangles so that the grain lines run vertically and horizontally. Keeping the fabric grain straight stabilizes the quilt, prevents sagging, and allows the borders to attach more easily.

Corner Triangles

Corner triangles are made from a square cut diagonally in one direction so that one square yields two corner (half-square) triangles. To calculate the size of square needed, divide the finished block size by 1.414 and add .875" (⅞") for seam allowances. Round this to the nearest ⅛".

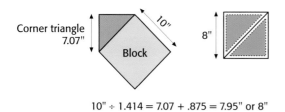

10" ÷ 1.414 = 7.07 + .875 = 7.95" or 8"

Side Triangles

Side triangles are made from a square cut diagonally in two directions so that one square yields four side (quarter-square) triangles. To calculate the size of square needed, multiply the finished block size by 1.414 and add 1.25 (1¼") for seam allowances. Round this to the nearest ⅛".

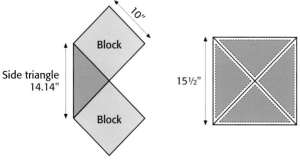

10" x 1.414 = 14.14" + 1.25 = 15.39" or 15½"

The following chart gives measurements of side and corner triangles for the most common quilt-block sizes. However, you may prefer to over-cut your squares by ½" to 1" and then trim them down once your top is pieced together.

FINISHED BLOCK SIZE	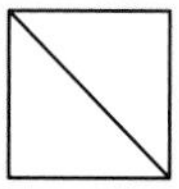 CUT SQUARE SIZE OF CORNER TRIANGLE	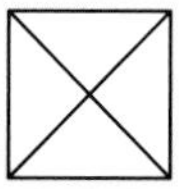 CUT SQUARE SIZE OF SIDE TRIANGLE
2" block	2⅜"	4⅛"
3" block	3"	5½"
4" block	3¾"	7"
5" block	4½"	8⅜"
6" block	5⅛"	9¾"
7" block	5⅞"	11¼"
8" block	6⅝"	12⅝"
9" block	7¼"	14"
10" block	8"	15½"
12" block	9⅜"	18¼"
14" block	10⅞"	21⅛"
16" block	12¼"	23⅞"
18" block	13⅝"	26¾"
20" block	15⅛"	29⅝"
24" block	17⅞"	35¼"

YARDAGE REQUIREMENTS FOR PIECING

The following chart is based on a 40" usable width of fabric. Most 100% cotton fabrics used for quilt-making are between 42" and 44" wide, but after preshrinking and trimming off the selvages I consider anything over 40" a bonus. So, you might get a few more pieces than I've estimated, but you won't come up short.

Even though this chart gives yardage requirements for squares only, it can easily be used for other shapes. To determine how much yardage you'd need for half-square triangles, multiply the number of squares in the chart by two. To determine how much yardage you'd need for quarter-square triangles, multiply the number of squares by four.

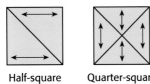

Half-square Triangles   Quarter-square Triangles

Arrows indicate straight of grain.

For rectangles, figure how many will fit into a square of a certain size and calculate from there.

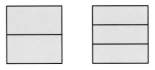

Two Rectangles   Three Rectangles

For irregular shapes, figure how many will fit into a square of a certain size and calculate from there.

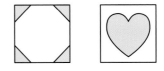

YARDAGE CHART FOR SQUARES

CUT SIZE OF SQUARE	FINISHED SIZE OF SQUARE	YARDAGE NEEDED (40" OF USABLE FABRIC)							
		¼ YD.	½ YD.	¾ YD.	1 YD.	1¼ YDS.	1½ YDS.	1¾ YDS.	2 YDS.
1½"	1"	130	286	416	572	702	858	1066	1144
2"	1½"	80	160	240	320	400	480	620	640
2½"	2"	48	96	160	224	272	320	400	448
3"	2½"	26	65	104	143	195	221	260	286
3½"	3"	22	55	77	110	132	165	187	220
4"	3½"	20	40	60	80	110	130	150	170
4½"	4"	8	27	40	56	72	88	104	112
5"	4½"	8	24	40	56	64	80	96	112
5½"	5"	7	21	28	42	56	63	77	84
6"	5½"	6	12	24	30	42	48	60	66
6½"	6"	6	12	24	30	36	48	54	66
7½"	7"	5	10	15	20	25	35	40	45
8½"	8"	4	8	12	16	20	24	28	32
9½"	9"		4	8	12	16	20	24	28
10½"	10"		3	6	9	12	15	15	18
11½"	11"		3	6	9	9	12	15	18
12½"	12"		3	6	6	9	12	15	15
13½"	13"		2	4	4	6	8	8	10
14½"	14"		2	2	4	6	6	8	8
15½"	15"		2	2	4	4	6	8	8
16½"	16"		2	2	4	4	6	6	8
17½"	17"		2	2	4	4	6	6	8
18½"	18"			2	2	4	4	6	6
19½"	19"			2	2	4	4	6	6

YARDAGE REQUIREMENTS FOR BINDING

The yardage requirements given here are based on binding that is made from a 2"-wide strip of fabric. Decide if you want to cut your strips on the straight of grain or on the bias. Bias strips take slightly more fabric; however, the yardage given is ample for either straight-grain or bias strips. Binding strips cut 2" wide can be used for a traditional single-layer binding with a finished width of ½".

For a double-layer French binding, fold 2¼"-wide strips in half lengthwise, wrong sides together. Then stitch the raw edges to the quilt and the remaining folded edge to the back of the quilt. The finished width will be approximately ⅜".

Determine the distance around your quilt and add about 20" for turning corners and seaming the binding strips together into a continuous piece. Round this number up to the nearest yard to determine the length of the binding strip.

LENGTH OF BINDING	FABRIC NEEDED
4 yards	¼ yard
6 yards	⅓ yard
8 yards	½ yard
10 yards	⅔ yard
12 yards	¾ yard
16 yards	1 yard

YARDAGE REQUIREMENTS FOR BACKING

If 42"-wide fabric is used, the backing for most quilts larger than crib size needs to be pieced together from two or more strips of fabric. The piecing seams can run horizontally or vertically, as long as the fabric isn't a directional print. To back large quilts and eliminate the necessity of piecing the backing, look for 90"-wide, 100% cotton fabric, available in solids and prints. Avoid the temptation to use a bed sheet for backing, because sheets can be difficult to quilt through.

If you're planning to put a hanging sleeve or rod pocket on the back of your quilt, you may need to purchase a little extra backing fabric so that the sleeve and backing match. Once you know the finished size of your quilt, refer to the following diagrams to plan the backing layout and to determine how much fabric is required. Be sure to trim off the selvages before stitching the seams.

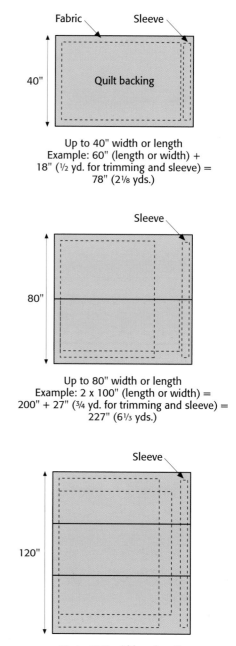

Up to 40" width or length
Example: 60" (length or width) +
18" (½ yd. for trimming and sleeve) =
78" (2⅛ yds.)

Up to 80" width or length
Example: 2 x 100" (length or width) =
200" + 27" (¾ yd. for trimming and sleeve) =
227" (6⅓ yds.)

Up to 120" width or length
Example: 3 x 100" (length or width) =
300" + 36" (1 yd. for trimming and sleeve) =
336" (9⅓ yds.)

Resources

QUILTMAKING SOFTWARE

For more information on quiltmaking software, contact your local quilt shop or contact the following businesses.

The Electric Quilt Company

419 Gould Street, Suite 2
Bowling Green OH 43402-3047
Phone: 1-800-356-4219
Fax: (419) 352-4332
Email: sales@electricquilt.com
Web: www.electricquilt.com

Quilt-Pro Systems, Inc.

PO Box 560692
The Colony, TX 75056
Phone: 800-884-1511
Fax: (972) 625-4240
Web: www.quiltpro.com

QUILTMAKING GUIDE

Directions for making the quilts shown in this book can be found in the Martingale & Company publications listed below. Contact your local quilt shop or refer to the back of this book to order directly from Martingale & Company.

Page 9: "Millennium Star" from *Nickel Quilts: Great Designs from 5-Inch Scraps* by Pat Speth and Charlene Thode

Page 10: "Stars and Stripes" from *Patriotic Little Quilts* by Alice Berg, Sylvia Johnson, and Mary Ellen Von Holt

Page 11: "White and Blue, Old and New" from *The Simple Joys of Quilting: 30 Timeless Quilt Projects* by Joan Hanson and Mary Hickey

Page 11: "Daniel's Boon" from *Scrap Frenzy: Even More Quick-Pieced Scrap Quilts* by Sally Schneider

Page 12: "Sunshine and Shadow" from *Beyond the Blocks: Quilts with Great Borders* by Nancy J. Martin

Page 13: "Perkiomen Valley in the 1930s" from *Scrap Frenzy: Even More Quick-Pieced Scrap Quilts* by Sally Schneider

Page 13: "Winter in the Cabin" from *The Joy of Quilting* by Joan Hanson and Mary Hickey

Page 14: "Beach Blues" from *The Simple Joys of Quilting: 30 Timeless Quilt Projects* by Joan Hanson and Mary Hickey

Page 14: "Cheerful Child" from *The Joy of Quilting* by Joan Hanson and Mary Hickey

Page 15: "North Wind" from *The Simple Joys of Quilting: 30 Timeless Quilt Projects* by Joan Hanson and Mary Hickey

Page 15: "Flying Geese Fishing Quilt" from *Cutting Corners: Quilts with Stitch-and-Trim Triangles* by Joan Hanson

Page 16: "Garden Comfort" from *Bed and Breakfast Quilts: With Rise and Shine Recipes* by Mimi Dietrich

Page 16: "Pennsylvania Flower Garden" from *Artful Album Quilts: Appliqué Inspirations from Traditional Blocks* by Jane Townswick

Page 17: "Mark's Nine Patch" from *The Simple Joys of Quilting: 30 Timeless Quilt Projects* by Joan Hanson and Mary Hickey

Page 18: "Maggie's Quilt" from *Triangle-Free Quilts* by Judy Hopkins

Page 18: "Kids in the Corner" from *The Simple Joys of Quilting: 30 Timeless Quilt Projects* by Joan Hanson and Mary Hickey

Page 19: "Wonder Baby" from *Sweet and Simple Baby Quilts* by Mary Hickey

Page 19: "Barbie's Baskets" from *Cutting Corners: Quilts with Stitch-and-Trim Triangles* by Joan Hanson

Page 20: "Red Union Square" from *The Simple Joys of Quilting: 30 Timeless Quilt Projects* by Joan Hanson and Mary Hickey

Page 20: "Old Fashioned Churn Dash" from *The Simple Joys of Quilting: 30 Timeless Quilt Projects* by Joan Hanson and Mary Hickey

Page 21: "My Heart Belongs to the '30s" from *Threads from the '30s: Quilts Using Reproduction Fabrics* compiled by Nancy J. Martin

Page 21: "Winter Lilies" from *Potting Shed Patchwork: 14 Quilted Projects Fresh from the Garden* compiled by Nancy J. Martin

Page 22: "Gabriel Meets Dick and Jane" from *The Simple Joys of Quilting: 30 Timeless Quilt Projects* by Joan Hanson and Mary Hickey

Page 23: "Batik Nine Patch" from *Cutting Corners: Quilts with Stitch-and-Trim Triangles* by Joan Hanson

Page 23: "Garden Path" from *Cutting Corners: Quilts with Stitch-and-Trim Triangles* by Joan Hanson

Page 24: "Scottish Chain" from *The Simple Joys of Quilting: 30 Timeless Quilt Projects* by Joan Hanson and Mary Hickey

Page 24: "Chickens in the Chimney" from *The Joy of Quilting* by Joan Hanson and Mary Hickey

Page 24: "The Permanent Incomplete" from *The Simple Joys of Quilting: 30 Timeless Quilt Projects* by Joan Hanson and Mary Hickey

Page 25: "Breakfast in Bed" from *The Joy of Quilting* by Joan Hanson and Mary Hickey

Page 25: "Topsy Turvy Hearts" from *Sweet and Simple Baby Quilts* by Mary Hickey

Page 25: "Cherry Star Picnic" from *Cutting Corners: Quilts with Stitch-and-Trim Triangles* by Joan Hanson

Page 26: "Kelley's Quilt," from *Cutting Corners: Quilts with Stitch-and-Trim Triangles* by Joan Hanson

Page 26: "Women in the Men's Club" from *The Joy of Quilting* by Joan Hanson and Mary Hickey

Page 27: "Purple Passion" from *The Simple Joys of Quilting: 30 Timeless Quilt Projects* by Joan Hanson and Mary Hickey

Page 27: "Swedish Stepping Stars" from *The Simple Joys of Quilting: 30 Timeless Quilt Projects* by Joan Hanson and Mary Hickey

Page 28: "Happy Birthday Baby" from *Celebrations!: Quilts for Cherished Family Moments* by Mary M. Covey

Page 28: "Redwork Airedales" from *Christmas Cats and Dogs: Quilts to Celebrate the Season* by Janet Kime

Page 29: "Tillie's Posy Pots" from *The Simple Joys of Quilting: 30 Timeless Quilt Projects* by Joan Hanson and Mary Hickey

Page 29: "It All Started with Ralph's Mother" from *The Joy of Quilting* by Joan Hanson and Mary Hickey

Page 30: "Christmas Bear Paw" from *The Joy of Quilting* by Joan Hanson and Mary Hickey

Page 31: "Cabin in the Trees" from *Beyond the Blocks: Quilts with Great Borders* by Nancy J. Martin

Page 31: "Feedsack Flags" from *Patriotic Little Quilts* by Alice Berg, Sylvia Johnson, and Mary Ellen Von Holt

Page 32: "Big Dipper" from *Nickel Quilts: Great Designs from 5-Inch Scraps* by Pat Speth and Charlene Thode

Page 32: "Christmas Bulbs" from *Make Room for Christmas Quilts: Quilts and Decorating Ideas* from Nancy J. Martin

Page 33: "Hearts and Arrows" from *The Simple Joys of Quilting: 30 Timeless Quilt Projects* by Joan Hanson and Mary Hickey

Page 33: "Jelly Beans" from *Scrap Frenzy: Even More Quick-Pieced Scrap Quilts* by Sally Schneider

Page 34: "54-40 or Fight" from *Beyond the Blocks: Quilts with Great Borders* by Nancy J. Martin

Page 34: "Jewel Box" from *Cutting Corners: Quilts with Stitch-and-Trim Triangles* by Joan Hanson

Page 34: "Dutch Treat Dishes" from *Cutting Corners: Quilts with Stitch-and-Trim Triangles* by Joan Hanson

Page 35: "Friendship Stars" from *The Simple Joys of Quilting: 30 Timeless Quilt Projects* by Joan Hanson and Mary Hickey

Page 35: "Honeymoon Suite" from *Bed and Breakfast Quilts: With Rise and Shine Recipes* by Mimi Dietrich

Page 36: "Country Village" from *Cutting Corners: Quilts with Stitch-and-Trim Triangles* by Joan Hanson

Page 36: "Beary, Beary Strawberry" from *The Simple Joys of Quilting: 30 Timeless Quilt Projects* by Joan Hanson and Mary Hickey

Page 37: "Hollyhock Wreath" from *Threads from the '30s: Quilts Using Reproduction Fabrics* compiled by Nancy J. Martin

Page 37: No pattern given for "Irish Trip" from *Trip to Ireland: Quilts Combining Two Old Favorites* by Elizabeth Hamby Carlson.

Page 38: "English Rose" from *Potting Shed Patchwork: 14 Quilted Projects Fresh from the Garden* compiled by Nancy J. Martin

Page 38: "Dorothy's Garden Girls" from *Threads from the '30s: Quilts Using Reproduction Fabrics* compiled by Nancy J. Martin

Page 39: "Little Sweethearts" from *From the Heart: Quilts to Cherish* compiled by Dawn Anderson

Page 41: No pattern given for "Framed Four Patch" from *Patriotic Little Quilts* by Alice Berg, Sylvia Johnson, and Mary Ellen Von Holt

Page 43: "The Incredibly Cool Cosmic Rocket Ship" from *The Joy of Quilting* by Joan Hanson and Mary Hickey

Page 43: "Dad's Quilt" from *The Casual Quilter: 6 Stress-Free Projects* by Robin Strobel

Page 44: "Sunny Sailors" from *Sweet and Simple Baby Quilts* by Mary Hickey

Page 44: "Tilted Pinwheels" from *The Simple Joys of Quilting: 30 Timeless Quilt Projects* by Joan Hanson and Mary Hickey

Page 46: "A Garden of Hearts" from *Potting Shed Patchwork: 14 Quilted Projects Fresh from the Garden* compiled by Nancy J. Martin

Page 47: "Flower Bed" from *Quilts from Larkspur Farm* by Pamela Mostek and Jean Van Bockel

Page 48: "Dick and Jane's Christmas Flannel Quilt" from *Make Room for Christmas Quilts: Quilts and Decorating Ideas* from Nancy J. Martin

Page 48: No pattern available for "Too Fruity" by Joan Hanson.

Page 49: "Spring Flower Garden" from *Cutting Corners: Quilts with Stitch-and-Trim Triangles* by Joan Hanson

Page 49: "Andrew and Patrick Sail Away" from *The Simple Joys of Quilting: 30 Timeless Quilt Projects* by Joan Hanson and Mary Hickey

Page 50: "Garland Star" from *The Joy of Quilting* by Joan Hanson and Mary Hickey

Page 50: "Kristen's Four Patch" from *The Simple Joys of Quilting: 30 Timeless Quilt Projects* by Joan Hanson and Mary Hickey

Page 51: "Fantastic Fans and Beautiful Bows" from *The Joy of Quilting* by Joan Hanson and Mary Hickey

Page 51: "Wiggle Flowers" from *Sweet and Simple Baby Quilts* by Mary Hickey

Page 52: "Little Shoo Fly" from *Cutting Corners: Quilts with Stitch-and-Trim Triangles* by Joan Hanson

Page 53: "Holly Berry Wreath" from *Cutting Corners: Quilts with Stitch-and-Trim Triangles* by Joan Hanson

Page 54: "Larkspur Farm Quilt" from *Quilts from Larkspur Farm* by Pamela Mostek and Jean Van Bockel

Page 55: "Line Dancing Lilies" from *The Joy of Quilting* by Joan Hanson and Mary Hickey

About the Author

JOAN HANSON MADE HER FIRST QUILT at the age of ten for her Barbie doll, and that started a lifelong passion for sewing and quiltmaking. Later, Joan began her education career by teaching high-school home-economics classes. In more recent years, she's been teaching quilting classes locally as well as around the country. She is the author of the best-selling book *Cutting Corners: Quilts Made with Stitch-and-Trim Triangles* and the co-author, with Mary Hickey, of *The Simple Joys of Quilting: 30 Timeless Quilt Projects*. In addition to quilting, Joan enjoys spending time at her family's cabin on Whidbey Island, walking the beach, digging clams, and pulling crab pots.